Epu

General Editor
Ivor H. Jones

The Book of Deuteronomy

Epworth Commentaries
Already published
The Book of Exodus
Richard Coggins
The Book of Job
C.S. Rodd
Isaiah 1–39
David Stacey
The Book of Ezekiel
Charles Biggs
The Books of Amos and Hosea
Harry Mowvley
The Gospel of Matthew
Ivor H. Jones
The Gospel of Luke
Judith Lieu
The Gospel of John
Kenneth Grayston
The Acts of the Apostles
James D.G. Dunn
The Epistle to the Romans
Kenneth Grayston
The First Epistle to the Corinthians
Nigel Watson
The Second Epistle to the Corinthians
Nigel Watson
The Epistle to the Galatians
John Ziesler
The Epistle to the Ephesians
Larry J. Kreitzer
The Epistle to the Philippians
Howard Marshall
The Epistle to the Colossians
Roy Yates
The Pastoral Epistles
Margaret Davies
The Epistle to the Hebrews
Paul Ellingworth
The Epistle of James
Michael J. Townsend
The Epistles of Peter and Jude
David C. Horrell
The Johannine Epistles
William Loader
Revelation
Christopher Rowland

The Book of DEUTERONOMY

A Preacher's Commentary

Ronald E. Clements

EPWORTH PRESS

Copyright © Ronald E. Clements 2001

British Library Cataloguing in Publication Data

A catalogue record of this book is available
from the British Library

0 7162 0543 2

First published 2001
by Epworth Press
20 Ivatt Way
Peterborough, PE3 7PG

Typeset by Regent Typesetting, London
and printed in Great Britain by
Biddles Ltd, Guildford and King's Lynn

CONTENTS

GENERAL INTRODUCTION

The *Epworth Preacher's Commentaries* that Greville P. Lewis edited so successfully in the 1950s and 1960s having now served their turn, the Epworth Press has commissioned a team of distinguished academics who are also preachers and teachers to create a new series of commentaries that will serve readers into the twenty-first century. We have taken the opportunity offered by the publication in 1989 of the Revised English Bible to use this very readable and scholarly version as the basis of our commentaries, and we are grateful to the Oxford and Cambridge University Presses for the requisite licence and for granting our authors generous access. They will nevertheless be free to cite and discuss other translations wherever they think that these will illuminate the original text.

Just as the books that make up the Bible differ in their provenance and purpose, so our authors will necessarily differ in the structure and bearing of their commentaries. But they will all strive to get as close as possible to the intention of the original writers, expounding their texts in the light of the place, time, circumstances, and culture that gave them birth, and showing why each work was received by Jews and Christians into their respective Canons of Holy Scripture. They will seek to make full use of the dramatic advance in biblical scholarship world-wide but at the same time to explain technical terms in the language of the common reader, and to suggest ways in which Scripture can help towards the living of a Christian life today. They will endeavour to produce commentaries that can be used with confidence in ecumenical, multiracial, and multifaith situations, and not by scholars only but by preachers, teachers, students, church members, and anyone who wants to improve his or her understanding of the Bible.

Ivor H. Jones

ix

ABBREVIATIONS

AB	Anchor Bible
AV	Authorised Version 1611
BCE	Before the Common Era
CE	Common Era
Eng. Tr.	English Translation
ICC	International Critical Commentary
NCB	New Century Bible Commentaries
NIB	New Interpreter's Bible
NIBC	New International Bible Commentaries
NICOT	New International Commentary on the Old Testament
NIV	New International Version, 1979
NRSV	New Revised Standard Version, 1989
OBT	Overtures to Biblical Theology
REB	Revised English Bible, 1989

BIBLIOGRAPHY

Clements, R. E., *Deuteronomy*, NIB, Vol. 2, pp. 269–538, Nashville, 1998.

Craigie, P. C., *The Book of Deuteronomy*, NICOT, 1976.

Driver, S. R., *Deuteronomy*, ICC 3rd edition Edinburgh, 1902.

Harrelson, Walter, *The Ten Commandments and Human Rights*, OBT, Philadelphia, 1980.

Lohfink, N., *Theology of the Pentateuch: Themes of the Priestly Narrative and Deuteronomy*, Eng. Tr., Minneapolis, 1994.

Mayes, A. D. H., *Deuteronomy*, NCB, London, 1979.

Miller, P. D., *Deuteronomy*, Interpretation Commentaries, Louisville, 1990.

Niditch, Susan, *War in the Hebrew Bible. A Study in the Ethics of Violence*, Oxford, 1993.

Olson, D. T., *Deuteronomy and the Death of Moses*, OBT, Minneapolis, 1994.

Weinfeld, M., *Deuteronomy and the Deuteronomic School*, Oxford, 1972.

—— *Deuteronomy 1–11*, New York, 1991.

Wright, C. J. H., *Deuteronomy*, NIBC, Carlisle, 1996.

—— *God's People in God's Land. Family, Land and Property in the Old Testament*, Exeter, 1990.

INTRODUCTION

Reading Deuteronomy today

The book of Deuteronomy appears as the fifth of the books ascribed to Moses which go to make up the Pentateuch, or 'Law', of the Old Testament. Its name means 'second law' and is taken from the Greek translation of Deut. 17. 18 which refers to a copy, or 'repetition', of the law of Moses given in the first instance on Mount Sinai, the sacred mountain to which the Israelites fled after escaping from their enforced slavery in Egypt. The mountain is regularly called Horeb in Deuteronomy – one of the features which indicates that the authors of it reflect a very carefully co-ordinated and planned body of ideas, language and historical traditions. This fact makes the book the most easily recognized and unified of those in the Pentateuch, and indeed, of the Old Testament as a whole. Deuteronomy has aptly been described as the 'centre' of the Old Testament on account of the emphasis it places on themes and ideas which subsequently dominate the Bible throughout.

Central among these themes is the claim that there is, and can be, only one God (monotheism), all other claims being bogus and mistaken (but see commentary on 6. 4). Secondly it affirms that the worship of false gods is chiefly expressed in various forms of idolatry and this false worship is the major cause of sinful and destructive human behaviour and lifestyles. So right thinking about God is fundamental to right dealing with fellow human beings. The one true God has no visible form, and must not therefore be represented by carved or pictorial images, whether of human beings or animals, the worship of things, or creatures, being a dangerous denial of the truth that God's existence extends above and beyond the material and physical realms of earth (transcendence).

In turn this carefully thought through theology is interwoven with an extensive set of laws which show how a divinely approved lifestyle is to be conducted. These laws are, in turn, reinforced by homilies and exhortations offering a most remarkable and perceptive emphasis upon the inwardness of faith and obedience. This emphasis is summed up in the enduring demand for love of God as the focus of all human duty and worship. In line with this concern with the inward and spiritual nature of worship are guidelines and rules for the organization and conduct of public worship. Rituals and services are to be matched with appropriate personal attitudes and reflections relating to God and the human situation. All told it would be difficult to imagine an Old Testament, or the Jewish and Christian religions deriving from it, which did not include the teaching of Deuteronomy, so basic and fundamental has its influence proved to be.

Deuteronomy in the Bible

In a more formal analysis Deuteronomy conveys a 'second giving' of the laws of Horeb (Sinai). These are presented in a series of addresses by Moses to the survivors of the Hebrew fugitives from Egypt on the eve of their entry into the land promised to their ancestors Abraham, Isaac and Jacob. Thirty-eight years had elapsed since the laws were first given. A new generation had grown up and Moses was close to death, being forewarned that he would not himself live to enter the land. This theme is important to Deuteronomy since it highlights the feature that Moses is presented as the greatest of Israel's leaders – greater than kings, priests, or even prophets, and yet the people must prepare themselves for life without him. How are they to do this? The answer lies not in setting up a succession of leaders who will follow Moses, although Joshua, and an approved order of judges and prophets, will partly do so and will help to fill the gap. But none can wholly do so, with the consequence that the primary source of guidance for the future must rest in the book of law, or more properly 'instruction' – Deuteronomy – which Moses provided for the nation in days to come. After Moses Israel would be ' the people of a book'.

With Deuteronomy therefore Israel became the possessors of a Bible, not of course in the full later sense of the Bible as Jews and Christians have received it, but in the essential focus that the revelation of God for future generations of Israel had been given in a written book. God's truth would be preserved in writing, and would in this fashion not be vulnerable to the whims and uncertainties occasioned by human followers of tradition. The law would be a constant witness to God's truth given through Moses.

The core of this revelation is to be found in the Ten Commandments which are repeated in Deut. 5. 6–21, having originally been revealed in Exod. 20. 2–17. In turn these commandments form the framework, or headings, for the more formal set of laws governing worship and civil justice contained in Deut. 12. 1–26. 15. The Ten Commandments form a kind of 'law within a law', and are not in themselves properly laws at all (they prescribe no explicit punishments). They are rather principles, or guidelines, which have quite usefully been compared to a declaration of human rights. So the laws of Deut. 12–26 can be viewed as an elaboration, or outworking, of the principles of the commandments. Nor is it difficult to understand that such commandments would need to be further elaborated and applied, which is very much how both Jews and Christians have understood them. For Christians the Ten Commandments provide an outline summary of God's law. For Jews a formal 'Code of Practice' summarizing the rules and guidelines of God's law was compiled in post-biblical times (third to fifth centuries CE) in the Mishnah (= 'second'[law]). This extends yet further the principle established in Deuteronomy of elaborating in more detail a core of basic divine commands. By studying Deuteronomy therefore we are face to face with one of the most central, and formative, features of both Jewish and Christian faith.

Deuteronomy as a book

From a literary perspective Deuteronomy brings the Pentateuch to a close and serves to round off the structure of these five basic books. These are now joined to form one single continuous narrative, but were evidently built up from various units, chiefly stories of Israel's ancestors interspersed with laws and religious directions. This final shaping of the Pentateuch was itself closely linked to the composition of Deuteronomy, so clearly is it designed to be the final chapter telling of the founding era of the Hebrew Bible. Afterwards, from the book of Joshua onwards, the story unfolds to tell a more varied tale of Israel's fortunes, illustrating high-points and low ones, judged according to the degree of faith and obedience Israel displayed. It is the Pentateuch that lays the foundation of the Hebrew Bible so that the books of the Prophets and all the remainder build on this foundation. Since Deuteronomy provides the concluding focus of the Pentateuch it serves very well as a guide to its central message and meaning. It is 'Israel's Book of Law' *par excellence*.

Even though Deuteronomy belongs inseparably to the Pentateuch, its influence, and the influence of its authors, can be viewed very powerfully in the way in which several other books of the Bible have been composed with a distinctive style and theological character reflecting the Deuteronomic spirit. Most to the fore here are the books of Judges and I and II Kings, but it is true also of the other historical books (Joshua, I and II Samuel) and the book of the prophet Jeremiah. All of these have been held to show strong 'Deuteronomic' (some scholars have preferred to use the adjective 'Deuteronomistic') influence on account of the similarities of language and spiritual emphasis which they show. Even in English translation these similarities can easily be noted by the careful reader. What they imply about the way in which the Hebrew Bible in its wholeness has been composed and put together has needed to be considered as a major subject of literary and historical investigation.

So far as its own structure and contents are concerned the various parts of which Deuteronomy is comprised are easily identified. The heart of the book is certainly to be found in the Ten Commandments of Deut. 5. 6–21 which provide a point of reference for all the remainder. Yet this series of commandments must certainly have been older than the present book of Deuteronomy and there exists a central law collection in Deut. 12. 1–25. 19 which is more usually thought of as the Deuteronomic law book. It has proved a helpful suggestion that the ordering of the laws in this collection follows the order of the Commandments, although identification of the precise sequence calls for some freedom and flexibility. In any case this law book cannot have been a law book in the modern sense of a precisely fixed book of civil and criminal laws, since there are many religious instructions set within it. The more directly legal material is chiefly in 19. 1–25. 19.

Alongside these laws, and preparing for them, is a historical introduction in chapters 1–3, followed by a series of speeches and sermons from Moses in chapters 4–11 in which the danger of not heeding the laws is forcefully spelt out. Similarly the temptation not to do so, as a mark of ordinary human weakness, is perceptively explored. For the modern reader it is these addresses which provide the most memorable teaching of the book, since they probe deeply into the nature of human sinfulness and reveal the heart of biblical spirituality. A series of warnings and poems in chapters 27–30 build around the theme of blessing and curse, re-emphasizing the Deuteronomic sense that human life is a question of choices and decision-making in which God can either be worshipped and obeyed, or rejected. The final epilogue in chapters 31–34 contains two long poems from Moses, celebrating the centrality of faith in God as the focus of life. They serve to bring the story of Moses' life and work to a close.

Deuteronomy as Christian Scripture

For the Christian, Deuteronomy must be viewed somewhat differently from the way it is in Judaism since, as the New Testament Pauline Epistles most strongly insist, the continued, and seemingly unlimited, elaboration of the divine law revealed through Moses could become oppressive. Its potential demands had no limit. Could then the whole range of the divine law ever be satisfied by human behaviour? Accordingly Christian concern with the Ten Commandments and with Deuteronomy has rightly recognized their central importance as basic writings dealing with God's law, but, at the same time, has expressed caution towards them. Christians must learn to see this law as a reality that needs to be viewed in the light of the teaching of Jesus in the Sermon on the Mount and the atonement secured by his death. Law and Gospel belong together and neither must be read, or understood, to the neglect of the other. Loving and serving God without obedience to the divine law would be meaningless. At the same time, trying to obey the law, without ever knowing that God accepted us in love in spite of our many failures, would be hopeless. So Law and Gospel, exhortations to serve and assurances of God's acceptance, belong together for the Christian, setting even such basic laws as those of Deuteronomy in a fresh perspective.

For the Christian Deuteronomy is also an unusually significant and meaningful book since it highlights what it means for the Christian to describe the Hebrew Bible as the *Old* Testament. It is not God's final word to us, but represents a provisional and incomplete revelation of divine truth which requires to be complemented by the fuller truth of the life and teaching of Jesus of Nazareth. So Deuteronomy, like the Old Testament as a whole, must be read discerningly and critically in the light of the teaching of Jesus Christ. Failure to do so can be, and sadly often has been, disastrous. It would be hard to find a book of the Old Testament where the importance of this principle of keeping a Christian perspective was more prominent and necessary than in reading and preaching Deuteronomy.

There are marked reasons for this which should be noted here, and then considered more fully in regard to specific passages of the book. First there is the fact that Deuteronomy is addressed to one small nation, or people, of Israel, whom it regards as uniquely chosen and privileged beyond all other peoples. When combined with the teaching on the oneness of God this gives rise to a picture of a God who is unfair and partisan in choosing only one from among the many peoples of the world. That God regards some people more favourably than others is contrary to the whole understanding of the divine nature (cf. Peter's declaration in Acts 10. 34–5 – God does not have favourites). In any case, such teaching quickly loses credibility. If there is indeed only one universal God, who is Creator and Sustainer of the world, then it would be incredible that the divine concern was only with one small part of humankind. The very idea of divine justice is challenged by such a belief. It is the New Testament which shows that belief in God's providential purpose, effective through human history, requires that particular peoples, with all their distinctive features, must be seen in the light of a divine plan for all human beings. Belief in one Creator God demands acknowledgement that all peoples on earth, throughout all ages, are recipients of an unmerited divine love. Particular peoples may serve a universal purpose.

The most tragically negative aspect of the doctrine of election in Deuteronomy is that it urges a policy of merciless genocide towards those peoples who are to be displaced by Israel from the Promised Land. There is much in Deuteronomy that breathes a spirit of intolerance which the Christian must oppose. The legacy of this, even to the present day, has been painful and terrifying. For Christians to emulate this can only be the result of failing to recognize the necessity of reading the Hebrew Scriptures in the light of the fuller revelation of God's love in Jesus Christ. This was clearly a major issue for Jesus himself and later for the apostle Paul. It should also be noted that Jewish tradition has also fully recognized the dangerous and unacceptable nature of this aspect of Deuteronomic teaching. It has consequently modified and reshaped it in the light of the wider range of biblical truth. The principle of interpreting Scripture by Scripture has proved both sound and necessary for Jews and Christians.

So far we have noted deficiencies and limitations which the Christian will find in Deuteronomy, sufficient perhaps to suggest to some that this book could now be ignored, or even repudiated as unhelpful and dangerous. Yet this is not the case, once the safeguards we have noted are kept in mind. Not only is the teaching of Deuteronomy a central plank of Judaism, but it has also served to shape Christian belief and devotion in a remarkable fashion. Of all the Old Testament writings it is that most often cited in the teaching of Jesus; it is that to which time and again the Early Church reverted in its desire to focus the most fundamental doctrines concerning God, humankind and the world.

Deuteronomy's emphasis upon a 'community of God' has been of great importance in human history and thought. It has given rise to the idea of a 'church' (the Greek word *ekklesia* is closely linked to the Old Testament idea of a covenant community) and in terms of social organization and lifestyle it has shown that faith without practical obedience to God is inadequate. The goal of a personal life of faith reaches out for expression in a divinely ordered community. So family life, social relationships, and even fundamental political and legal principles, all matter to faith since they shape the quality of a faith-*filled* life. Faith without social action would not be a true biblical faith. So Deuteronomy, more than any other Old Testament book, combines faith with practical rules and guidelines for life. It lays down spiritual principles and uncovers heart-searching insights which have shaped the biblical understanding of the religious life.

Deuteronomy's vocabulary of devotion and spiritual insight sets the biblical standard. The importance to worship of remembering, watching, and guarding against the deceitfulness of self-satisfaction and complacency mark out its rich contribution to human self-under-standing. The book of Deuteronomy is the biblical birthplace of many of these emphases so that it can still be richly rewarding to study them closely in this, their formative, setting.

What scholars say about Deuteronomy

From the perspective of two hundred years of careful investigation and research into the literary origin of Deuteronomy and how its teaching relates to that of other books of the Hebrew Bible two or three features stand out prominently. The first of these arises from awareness that it displays an aggressive, passionate and uncompro-mising nature, indicating its zeal for reform and religious purity. Central to this zeal is its demand that all formal worship must be cen-tralized at one single sanctuary, which has, at least since the days of David and Solomon, been identified with Jerusalem. This zeal for one pre-eminent place of worship is linked inseparably to the mainte-nance of consistency and purity of faith in Israel. This feature of the book associates it closely with the story of the great reform carried out by King Josiah in 622 BCE which is told in II Kgs. 22–23. Until this reform it is evident that in Israel demands for the centralization of worship either did not apply, or were largely ignored. This does not necessarily mean that they were not known, but it nevertheless is certain that the written book of Deuteronomy has much to do with Josiah's reform. The story of how, during restoration work on the

Jerusalem temple, the book of 'the law of Moses' (II Kgs. 22. 8–23. 3) was rediscovered introduces us in a very clear way to the existence of a book which had demands akin to central features of Deuteronomy. This does not prove that that book was Deuteronomy, as we know it, but quite evidently the scribes who produced Deuteronomy were very interested in the events that took place in Josiah's reign. This is what the story of the great reform at that time makes known to us. Since the laws of Deuteronomy very demonstrably revise the earlier lawbook of Exod. 20. 22–23. 19 (often called 'The Book of the Covenant') it is very plausible that it is this earlier book which featured prominently in Josiah's reform.

The fact that Deuteronomy is presented as a speech delivered by Moses on the eve of Israel's entry into the Promised Land, reveals its concern to preserve the most important features which had character-ized Israel's religion *from its beginning*. At the same time many aspects of the book's teaching reflect the setbacks and problems of the twilight years of the first great kingdom of Israel. Repeated and impassioned warnings indicate awareness that things had gone badly wrong for the kingdom that had once been so extensive under king David. Defeat and exile were staring Israel in the face. Occupation of the land is viewed with a wistful anxiety as a prize that was slipping from Israel's grasp. When we look closely we find several references to late events and consciousness of many defeats and their consequences in the book. Most especially are these found in the warnings and curses for those who are disobedient. There are repeated signs of a concern to arouse a sense of imminent danger and to set aside every vestige of complacency. The authors seek to revitalize and preserve the best of Israel's past in the face of an uncertain future. The very passion and eagerness to hold on to the teaching and law of Moses, and to make its demands clear and unmistakable, does little to hide the fear that this teaching, together with the land that God had promised to Israel's ancestors, might soon be lost.

Scholars have, with few serious exceptions, recognized that Deuteronomy was not, in its present form, written, or directly spoken, by Moses. It is a document which has striven to reclaim and refocus the central legacy of Moses' teaching for Israel in a way that shows every awareness that numerous temptations, misdirections and failures separated the nation, as it had become, from what Moses had intended it to be. A strong undercurrent shows that too much trust had been placed in the (Davidic) kingship, which had shown itself misplaced. Hence Moses is shown to be a greater leader than any king. Kingship itself is shown to be a questionable and dangerous institution. Over against the belief that a strong central administration could uphold principles of justice and law, Deuteronomy appeals to every family and every individual to recognize that reponsibility for justice and right conduct lies with them.

So a major scholarly conclusion from almost two centuries of research has been that, as a written document, Deuteronomy must have been composed, probably in a series of stages extending over almost a century, between Josiah's reign (639–609 BCE) and the middle of the next century, by which time the surviving kingdom of Judah had effectively collapsed.

The Deuteronomists introduce themselves, or at least the role which they saw themselves as fulfilling, at the beginning of their book in 1. 9–18. They were the disciples and heirs of Moses, entrusted from the days of that great leader, with the task of guiding and instructing Israel in matters of law. Yet what they offered is more than law in the narrower sense, since it is a comprehensive charter for a nation, embracing every aspect of its life – government, religion and worship, commerce and education, besides the administration of law. What began as a movement for reform, undertaken with partial success in Josiah's reign, finished up as a more far-reaching programme of hoped-for restoration for a nation that was on the point of disintegrating. This became reality when Judah, the last surviving part of the former kingdom, succumbed to Babylonian destruction in the first half of the sixth century BCE. The nation was all but finished and the Jewish dispersion among the nations had begun! So Deuteronomy is the document, above all others, which binds together a knowledge of Israel's past with a charter for its future. It is a handbook which aims to show how to live as 'the people of God' in lands and communities where such a way of life often appeared strange and foreign. With good reason some scholars have argued that Deuteronomy is the most central, because most typical, book of the entire Old Testament.

Time and place in Deuteronomy

It can be understood in this context that Moses is the figure who lends authority and significance to the book of Deuteronomy without, in the strict literary sense, being its author. Moreover, we discover that the timescale woven into the structure of the book fits this presentation of revealed authority very significantly. Israel is shown to remain the same throughout all its generations. Temptations and sins of the past recur and are repeated in the present. The challenges and opportunities faced by the first generation as they were about to set foot to cross the river Jordan were the same challenges that faced the present generation of the book's readers, and would face generations yet to come! The past had lessons to teach because its pitfalls and opportunities were still there for a new generation of readers to face. Past failures merely emphasised their importance. The reader is carried back to hear the call of Moses as though ripples of the Jordan's current could still be heard and were still to be crossed. The adventure of life under God's covenant was about to begin. In a spiritual sense this was true, and had remained true from the beginning.

In spelling out the problems and mistakes that the readers would have to avoid, the writer knew all too well how painfully these failures had, in the past, robbed the nation's predecessors of their spiritual heritage. So the key words of 'watch, remember, take care', reappear with a fervour born of experience. Deuteronomy is a remarkable work on account of its insistence that looking forward requires looking back.

The scholarly perception that Deuteronomy was not actually written by Moses, but rather is composed from a distillation of insights and truths based on his creative role as Israel's first great leader, instead of weakening our appreciation of its importance rather enhances it. Deuteronomy is the charter, or 'constitution' of a small, and relatively short-lived, nation of antiquity. It is really a short book, considering that it covers so many basic issues. Yet it is anything but a speculative or theoretical document. Rather it bears all the hallmarks of having tested in the fires of experience one of its own greatest truths *that people cannot live on bread alone, but they live on every word that comes from the mouth of the Lord* (Deut. 8. 3). Life is learning even more than it is possessing.

Deuteronomy and the preacher

Undoubtedly the foremost reason why the book of Deuteronomy offers a rich resource for the conscientious preacher lies in the fact that its own doctrines and concerns have led to the crystallization of fundamental truths in a range of clear and concise texts. It is a preacher's textbook. The sharp commandment form in which the writer addresses the reader shows a deep understanding of human psychology. It points to all too common temptations and addresses them with an authority based on experience and conviction. It has clearly been written by preachers and has been usefully summed up as a book of 'preached law' (Gerhard von Rad).

From the perspective of the preacher there is much to learn from Deuteronomy concerning the technique of preaching and sermon form. Instead of appealing for commitment to abstract principles the authors' imagination is employed skilfully to point to familiar situations and everyday contexts. There is no better illustration of this than in the well-known words which have come to be known as the *Shema* – 'Hear, O Israel ' (Deut. 6. 4–9). Instead of simply saying 'Keep this law always', the author pictures the varied situations of daily life – 'Recite them to your children . . . talk about them at home . . . and so on'. This technique of imaginative rhetorical admonition is splendidly developed in the great poems at the close of the book, picturing times of distress – even to the shame and horror of seeing one's own children sold in a slave market (cf. Deut. 28. 67–68). It uncovers feelings of despair in which the power and hope of Moses' words will take on a new meaning. The authors show themselves to be past masters in sensing the attitudes and responses of an audience which enables them to capture the reader's attention.

Much of the uniqueness of the Deuteronomic teaching lies in this ability to enter into the mind of the reader. Not only is there a deep awareness that most of the vital decisions that affect the quality of an individual's life lie deep down in the attitudes and desires of the human heart, but the authors are well aware how subtle and deceptive these can be. As preachers the authors can be said to 'know us better than we know ourselves'. Nor is there any complacent 'talking down' to the reader, since at many vital points the text uses the first-person plural form 'we . . . us' (e.g. in 1. 6, 19, etc.) to bring home a sense that the authors also share in the challenge, and all too often the failure, of responding to the call of God. Throughout there is commendable insight into the subtle powers of self-deception by which the people of God make excuses for themselves so that the full challenge of obedient response is overlooked. Even in the Psalms it is hard to find a greater emphasis upon the inwardness of faith and the inner demands of God's call than we find in Moses' sermons in Deuteronomy 5–9. This is undoubtedly the heartland of biblical spirituality with its interpretation of the goal of worship in terms that we still employ – 'Be strong . . . take courage . . . remember . . . watch out . . .'

Deuteronomy is a preacher's book in the fullest sense, and it is on this account that its classification as a book of law makes it doubly significant for the Christian. Most studies of the meaning of the Hebrew word *torah* point out that, besides meaning 'law' in the legal sense (there are many important laws of this nature in the book), it also means 'instruction'. It is one of the book's primary characteristics that it calls upon the reader to teach the central message of God's commandments in the home to children (Deut. 6. 7) and that it makes a great point of addressing itself to 'all Israel' (1. 1). Even when setting out rules for worship and the sorting out of legal matters, it does not lose this human, domestic flavour. In fact its sees faith and obedience to God as much a matter for the home as for the sanctuary. In sum it 'domesticates' the spiritual life!

A strong argument has been made that the ancient authors of the book appear to have been well versed in the needs and practice of education. Worship itself becomes a learning exercise, as well as a life-shaping encounter. There can be no true or lasting piety without knowledge, and this entails knowledge of the stories which highlight past human experience of God's reality. Obedience to God requires knowledge of the problems attendant upon firm and lasting human relationships. So the preaching style of Deuteronomy weaves together passionate appeals and exhortations, which could become tedious if repeated too often, with stories, poems and instructions which give colour and continuity to its message. It illustrates the law in action in order to demonstrate its principles. God's word, because it is *God's* word, calls for careful and practised presentation if it is to maintain the dignity which its claims to divine authority warrant.

Part I

A Preface to the Laws

1. 1–11. 32

Journey to the Promised Land
1. 1–3. 29

After a brief, and highly compressed, introduction to the book as a whole in 1. 1–5, the continuation in 1. 6–3. 29 is a narrative story of events that befell Israel during a thirty-eight year period (2. 14). This extended from the time of the departure from the mount of revelation, which Deuteronomy consistently calls Mount Horeb but is otherwise better known as Mount Sinai, until they reached the banks of the River Jordan (verses 1 and 5).

The introduction itself performs the essential task of scene-setting, locating the teaching of the book as the record of the words of Moses, given before the people had crossed the river to launch their attack upon the Promised Land. It serves in this fashion as a preparation for the story which unfolds in the book of Joshua, a book with which Deuteronomy is vitally connected. At the same time, however, the introductory stories of these chapters form a preparation for the reaffirmation of the central law contained in the Ten Commandments (chapter 5). They also prepare for the exposition of these commandments in a more directly legal fashion in chapters 12–26. So the introduction serves a dual purpose. It shows that an unwavering courage and commitment to the LORD as God will be necessary if the land promised to Abraham, Isaac and Jacob is to be won. It also shows the continued obedience that will be required thereafter if the land is to be retained as Israel's inheritance for future generations. So law and land are shown to belong together. They are interrelated gifts of God, one of them an unmerited gift of grace and the other the guide to a proper response to this grace showing that what God gives must be used responsibly and in trust. God takes the necessary steps to show how the unmerited treasures of life are to be used.

1

The stories that follow in 1. 6–3. 29 are divided into five separate episodes made up as follows:

1) The appointment of judges to assist Moses (1. 6–18)
2) The story of a reconnaissance of the land and its consequences (1. 19–46)
3) The crossing of the territory of the Edomites and Moabites (2. 1–7, 8–25)
4) The defeat of kings Sihon of Heshbon and Og of Bashan (2. 26–37; 3. 1–22)
5) Moses' request to enter the land and God's refusal (3. 23–29)

Introduction
1. 1–8

The careful establishing of the location of Moses' address to the people has been compiled from a variety of sources in order to present Israel as at the close of one phase of its early life and poised to begin another. The title 'all Israel' is widely used in the book, providing a strong emphasis to show that its message was, and remains, applicable to the entire nation without exception. The unity of Israel becomes a central theme, so that the subsequent break-up of the nation into two separate kingdoms (I Kgs. 12), was regarded as a major sin (cf. Isa. 7. 17).

The name *Horeb* is Deuteronomy's title for the holy mountain where the law was given to Moses, more familiarly called Sinai in the book of Exodus. It seems that the origin for the two names rests with Horeb being that of the region (the name signifies desolation), whereas Sinai was that of a particular mountain peak. The identification with the present-day *Jebel-Musa* ('The mountain of Moses') was not made with any certainty until the Christian period when St Jerome settled and worked there. The event of this revelation forms the central episode of the forty years spent by Israel in the wilderness after the deliverance from the slavery of service in Egypt. The law code of Deuteronomy is presented as essentially a recapitulation and reaffirmation of the original law-giving. Close examination shows that it represents a revision and up-dating of the provisions set out in the earlier law book of Exod. 20. 22–23. 19 (the 'Book of the Covenant'). If this earlier law code was instrumental in King Josiah's reform (II Kgs. 22–23), then the Book of Deuteronomy, in its completed form, was not finished until some time later, after the disasters of the sixth century had changed forever Israel's national existence.

2

Verse 2 gives an unusually precise calculation for a journey time with its reference to an eleven-day journey, and is unique in Deuteronomy. It is not wholly self-explanatory and such details over matters of calendar, time and itinerary are characteristic of the late Priestly tradition. Allowing two years for the journey to Mount Horeb, it had in reality taken Israel thirty-eight years to make this journey (cf. 2. 14–15). The eleven-day period for travel from the oasis at Kadesh-barnea to Horeb possibly derives from knowledge of slow-moving caravan-traders. Royal messengers travelled more swiftly and there are later hints of pilgrimages to the location (cf. I Kgs. 19. 8–9). These subsequently became important in the Christian period with the founding of the St Catherine's monastery at the presumed location. The victories over Sihon and Og (v. 4) are reported in Num. 21. 21–35.

The affirmation *'Moses resolved to expound this law'* (v. 5) fits well with the fact that many rulings in the Deuteronomic law code revise earlier provisions made in the Book of the Covenant (Exod. 20. 22–23. 19). So the claim that Moses 'expounded' the law takes on an added significance in that the laws are not simply repeated but elaborated and amended. The older text is taken to be in essential agreement with the revised presentation in Deuteronomy, so that the fundamental law itself remains unchanged, but required to be clarified. This principle of an expounding of the law lends to the title of Deuteronomy (a 'second law') an additional level of meaning. Such concern to amplify and build upon a basic text has remained fundamental for Jewish interpretation in the later Mishnah and Talmud.

The departure from Horeb and the decision to press on toward the land which had been promised to the ancestors (vv. 6–8) forms a vital starting point for Deuteronomy's historical preface. The delay in such a departure is interpreted as a consequence of the faint-heartedness and unbelief of those who first heard of the difficulties to be encountered in the land (1. 32–36; cf. Num. 13. 25–14. 45).

The appointment of judges
1. 9–18

The story of the appointment of officers, chosen from each of the tribes, has clearly been compiled with the help of two earlier narrative episodes which were available in written form to the author. The first of these in Num. 11. 10–25 deals with the appointment of seventy elders who were to assist in the administration of Israel because Moses was unable to carry the burden posed by the continued

3

demands and requests of the people. It is very striking that in this older narrative Moses indulges in a very angry and forthright prayer to God, setting out in no uncertain manner the impossibility of carrying the responsibility of caring for so large a group of people (cf. especially Num. 11. 10–15). He even dares God to put him to death, if there is to be no let up of the problem! As a result seventy elders are appointed to look after many of the day-to-day needs of the people. In illuminating fashion the author tells how God took some of the spirit that was in Moses and rested it on them (v. 25).

The second older narrative report is to be found in Exod. 18. 1–27 and tells how Moses, at the instigation of his father-in-law Jethro, selected chieftains from all the families of Israel to act as judicial officers. The number of them is not detailed, but they are to be responsible for hearing and judging disputes among the people, being appointed in a rather military fashion, to serve over them allocated by 'thousands, hundreds, fifties and tens' (Exod. 18. 25). The purpose of these officers is to relieve Moses of listening to, and adjudicating, minor disputes, leaving only the 'hard cases' for him to deal with.

The Deuteronomic account has combined the substance of the two reports, focusing primarily on the role of such appointed leaders as judges. The making of such appointments indicates that the choice was based on the known qualities of such persons as 'wise, discerning and reputable' (vv. 13, 15). They were clearly to be leaders from within each tribe to whom Moses delivers a firm admonition concerning the necessity for fairness and impartiality in passing judgement (v. 17). Significantly the author leaves out any indication that the original proposition for such an order of judicial officers was made by Jethro (Exod. 18. 1), instead merely noting that it came from Moses because the task was too great for one man to fulfil (Deut. 1. 9). It is a mark of the very high regard in which the account holds Moses that no mention is made of the angry prayer placed in his mouth by the earlier report.

From the perspective of understanding Deuteronomy and its spiritual outlook the episode is a very important one and is fittingly placed at the very beginning of the historical reports which summarize Israel's journey from Mount Horeb to the Plains of Moab. It seems highly likely that, in reporting such appointments at this early stage, the book is in fact introducing its own authors. The high level of concern with justice and wisdom focuses precisely on matters which are to the fore in Deuteronomy. Moreover in tracing back their authority to Moses (cf. especially v. 18) the report focuses directly on the one unique source of the book's authority. So it seems that here the book's authors introduce themselves to their readers, showing how and why, in this book, Moses still speaks to Israel.

Leadership and authority are two of the central issues it deals with. Who has authority to speak from God and where can spiritual leadership be found? That quality exemplified in the person of Moses provides the answer, and is focused on his own utter uniqueness as a man of God (cf. 34. 10). Equally relevant to such questions are a concern with bad, and even misguided, leadership. Accordingly the presentation of the source of the book's authority here, and the claim that it derives from Moses, is a vital key towards the interpretation of it.

The reconnaissance of the land
   1. 19–46

The prospect of, at last, venturing across the River Jordan and entering the Promised Land raises afresh concern with the reason why Israel had taken so long to make such a step. The story of how the Hebrews had sent out spies to reconnoitre the territory they were to occupy is told in detail in Num. 13–14 and is repeated here more briefly. Some significant changes of emphasis are made in the presentation of it, and its significance re-examined, since it reveals the people in their true colours. When first the reports were brought of the features of the land and its inhabitants, the majority of the nation became fear-struck and wished themselves back in the slavery of Egypt!

They were not men and women of great courage and faith. The issue then arose whether, thirty-eight years later, their children would show themselves to be made of sterner stuff. That past generation had wanted to take possession of the land promised to them by God but had been unwilling to accept the risks and dangers attendant on claiming it.

So the story of the spies is central to the message of Deuteronomy and brings to the surface an awareness of the underlying problems which the authors were addressing. After having introduced themselves as authors, they here turn to consider who their readers might be and the state of mind in which they were to be found. The problem is one of faith – faith in God and faith in the future. In turn it would also be a question of recovering faith in themselves. Did they identify with the generation that wilted when the report of the spies was made, or with those who were prepared to stake all on God and cross the River Jordan? The faith of Moses, Joshua and Caleb, contrasts starkly with the faithlessness of the rest of the people, who had now perished in the wilderness. Now a new generation were faced once again with the same choices.

Through and through Deuteronomy is a book about such human decision-making. In order to assist the reader to make the right choice, the issues are presented in the most forthright and dramatic manner possible. No one who today reads its warnings or summaries of past events can be in the slightest doubt as to where the authors' commitments lay. So the reader too must decide.

The passage through the territory of the Edomites
2. 1–7

The story of how the Hebrews made peaceful agreements with the Edomites is drawn and elaborated from the older account in Num. 20. 14–21. For their later ties with Israel cf. Deut. 23. 7–8, and this relationship is reflected in the concession of v. 6. Deuteronomy uses the name Esau, the brother of Israel's ancestor Jacob (cf. Gen. 33. 1–17), rather than Edom, although the names were originally separate. They were settled in the south to the east of the River Jordan, making them significant rivals for territory to Israel. The two names became virtually interchangeable, almost certainly as a result of conflicts and tribal unions which extended the Edomites borders (cf. Gen. 36. 40–43). The connection with the region of Seir (Gen. 36. 30) associates them also with the Horites (2. 12; cf. Gen. 36. 29). A list of their kings, noting that such kingship antedated the rise of kingship in Israel, is recorded in Gen. 36. 31–39. Edomite ethnic links appear to have been more Arab than Aramaean and their territory formed an eastern border for Judah, although the actual boundaries appear to have been constantly changing. The assertion that it was Israel's God who had given Mount Seir to the descendants of Esau (v. 5) reflects acceptance and resolution of territorial disputes which had incurred fierce conflicts in King David's reign (cf. II Sam. 8. 13–14).

The passage through the territory of the Moabites
2. 8–25

In order to maintain its own territorial claims, it was evidently very necessary to show where there were lands which did not form a part of Israel's inheritance. As the territory occupied by the Edomites was

6

accepted as rightfully theirs (2. 5), so also that of the Moabites was similarly recognized (2. 9). After their cruel subjugation in the time of King David (II Sam. 8. 1–2) the Moabites became important among Israel's neighbours. Yet for Israel to have entered the region west of the River Jordan required a passage through Moabite lands. Accordingly the report demonstrates that the Israelites conducted themselves as good and trustworthy neighbours by avoiding any conflict (v. 9). This was how Israel had behaved in the past and how it should continue to do so in the present by setting a good example.

A second issue of central Deuteronomic concern which is highlighted by these two reports concerns the need for, and goal of, warfare. This is focused almost exclusively upon the acquisition of territory. It is a sad feature of Deuteronomy, and its derivative literature such as the books of Joshua and Judges, that warfare looms very large on the author's horizon as a part of God's plans and activities affecting mankind. The consequences of this are more fully brought out in the episode which follows, but it is anticipated here. What becomes significant, although in no way removing the problem from a Christian moral perspective, is that warfare is regarded as necessary in order to secure and hold on to territory.

The defeat of king Sihon of Heshbon
2. 26–37

The reason for the battle that is now reported is very fully described (vv. 26–30). The battles are now reported which had been important victories for the Hebrews in the journey to take possession of the land. The older accounts of these battles are to be found in Num. 20. 12; 21. 21–31; 27. 12; 32. 1–42. Once again the Deuteronomic author weaves a smooth and connected story (notice the use of the first person plural form in 3. 1, 8 to show everybody's involvement in the action, which contrasts with the use of the first person singular by Moses) out of a rather disjointed and miscellaneous collection of reports. Its message is a clear and decisive one – where faith, obedience and trust in the leadership of Moses were present, then victory came swiftly and was assured.

A somewhat contrived point is made in 2. 26–30 which recognizes that seizure of another's territory can have no moral justification, but offers an explanation for Israel's doing so in the case of king Sihon of Heshbon. It asserts that reasonable terms for a negotiated passage were offered to the king by the Hebrews, but refused. As a result of this unfriendly action by Sihon his inevitable defeat by the Hebrews entailed that his land fell forfeit to the tribes of Israel. A ruling demanding that warfare against towns and cities should begin with an offer of peace – on humiliating terms – is to be found in 20. 10–14. If this offer is rejected and the city is captured, then all its contents are regarded as forfeit. Verse 30 interprets Sihon's action as part of the mysterious providence of God.

The defeat of king Og of Bashan
3. 1–11

There can be no softening of the intensity of the moral affront posed by the Deuteronomic theology of warfare by insisting that it was primarily a concern for defensive wars aimed at the protection and retention of Israel's land from invaders and marauders. Quite certainly by the time, and in the circumstances, in which the present book was completed this was largely the case. Nevertheless it must still be noted that a much more aggressive and unlimited form of warfare for the sake of conquest is what is actually advocated.

In similar fashion there can be little comfort and alleviation of the severity of the Deuteronomic demands by pointing out that in the actual historical events which marked Israel's occupation of the land, it is quite certain that such a wholesale genocide of the previous inhabitants did not take place. There is nonetheless abundant evidence that the prevalent lifestyle of the period was often uncompromisingly cruel. Much of the earliest Israelite occupation of Canaanite territory was through a prolonged and piecemeal process of infiltration, sometimes winning over the local communities to a new political allegiance. Deuteronomy, however, for reasons of its own, is deeply concerned to advocate a picture of a swift, violent and merciless campaign of conquest. Much still remains clouded in uncertainty as to the reasons which underlie this Deuteronomic viewpoint and who exactly the authors of the book saw to be the contemporary representatives of the Canaanites, whose continued survival elicited so much of their venom and hatred.

Generations of Christians have sought to find a surer moral purpose and character in this Deuteronomic theology of violence by translating it into a picture of a purely spiritual warfare (cf. John Bunyan's *The Holy War Made by Shaddai upon Diabolus* where Bunyan makes extensive use of his own experiences in the English Civil War). The enemies that are to be overthrown are the powerful forces of vice, deceit and corruption. Only by such an allegorical reinterpretation of such teaching can any moral value be rescued from it. Deuteronomy calls for courage, faith and steadfastness of purpose which can then be given a worthier goal than the harsh perspective that a properly literal and historical understanding of such stories and injunctions demands. Certainly when taken in their literal meaning they provide a salutary warning for the modern reader of the book to reflect on the dangers of misdirected religious zeal and the consequences of neglect of the universality of the Christian demand for love and compassion.

Territorial claims in Transjordan
3. 12–22

The territory on the eastern side of the River Jordan was both rich and fertile, with the added significance that it fulfilled an important role in maintaining control over the water supply of the river. It was also the natural route for trade between Mesopotamia and Egypt. It is small wonder then that the Deuteronomic authors cast a positive glance in the direction of this territory (vv. 12–17). In their eyes it had once formed a part of Greater Israel where the tribes of Reuben and Gad were settled together with a part of the tribe of Manasseh. It may be held as highly probable that these tribal settlements had once formed a part of Israel, and it mattered greatly to the Deuteronomic authors to retain a memory of that fact. From this tradition they endeavoured to maintain their claim upon it as part of the land promised to the ancestors.

It is, at the same time, evident that Israel's hold over these lands did not last long and that the natural boundary formed by the River Jordan and the weakened condition of Israel after the death of King Solomon meant that the tribes settled there quickly fell away in their political allegiance. Consequently there is little information preserved in the Old Testament concerning their fate. Reuben and Gad become tribes that virtually disappeared from historical record. The basis for the retention of this territorial claim by the Deuteronomists to a region which had largely ceased to play any effective role in the internal politics of the nation is unclear. Tradition, built around historical memory of Israel's greatness under King David, may have played some part in this, but it is also possible that, under Assyrian sovereignty, the Israelite cities of Shechem, Bethel and Gilgal were expected to maintain some administrative control over the region.

The second issue that surfaces in this summarizing tradition (vv.

18–22) concerns the military obligations that rested upon every section of the nation to participate in the military commitments of the whole. This conforms to the Deuteronomic understanding that Israel would field a conscript army, the obligations of which were determined by the relevant authorities (cf. 20. 1–20). The officers responsible for conscription referred to in 20. 5 would then have been assigned the tribal and territorial range of their duties. In this, as in a number of its prescriptions, Deuteronomy appears to be familiar with the formal and bureaucratic aspects of Assyrian administrative procedures, which it applies in a strongly nationalist direction. It was a fundamental conviction of its authors that Israel was one nation and that each of its members shared a common destiny. On one side this endorsed important privileges of status and equality, even for the most marginalized of its citizens (cf. the need for defining membership of the community in 23. 1–8). On the other side, there could be no privilege without responsibility and it is the military aspects of this which are set out in 3. 18–20.

Overall Deuteronomy offers strong evidence that Israel had learnt much, both good and bad, from the long period spent under Assyrian domination. On the positive side were skills and techniques of administration and political control. On the more negative side stood the oppressive and ultimately destructive aspects of foreign rule and tribute exactions. The Deuteronomic authors can best be understood as citizens who were prepared to adopt and use the administrative skills that had been learned from Mesopotamia in order to ensure that Israel would never again surrender its spiritual birthright to a foreign power. In the Deuteronomic world of thought allegiance to the LORD God of Israel became an ultimate and absolute requirement. By making that commitment the community could never again abandon this to serve any purely earthly ruler.

Moses' request and its refusal
   3. 23–29

The final narrative episode of the events leading up to the second giving of the law through Moses concerns the position of the great leader himself. It tells how Moses, now viewed as at the very height of his powers of leadership, prayed to God to be allowed to accompany his people into the Promised Land (v. 25). There is a certain logic in such a request since it was the generation which had shown itself so fainthearted which had condemned itself to death in the wilderness, while the faithful and courageous Joshua and Caleb, like Moses himself, had been in favour of going forward. They would not have wasted the thirty-eight years spent in the wilderness. If Moses was, from a human point of view, the architect and founder of the people of Israel, surely of all men he deserved to be present in the land which Israel was to occupy. Yet this had quite evidently not been the case, as Israel's own historical traditions affirmed (cf. Deut. 32. 48–52; 34. 5–8). Moses was a figure of the wilderness years, pointing Israel forward to a success and security which he himself was never destined to enjoy. We have already pointed out that this was a matter of great importance to the authors of Deuteronomy since, in a remarkable way, it tied in with the very character and purpose of the book. These authors show themselves intensely committed to celebrating and magnifying the importance of the figure of Moses for the life of Israel as a people. That Moses had never set foot in the Promised Land provided a way of drawing attention to the importance of Deuteronomy as his legacy and charter for Israel as the people to whom the land was given. Troubles and failures in the land arose because the people had neglected the teaching and warnings which Moses, the greatest of their leaders, had given to them. By the time the Deuteronomic law book was completed Israel had had many leaders, among them prophets of the stature of Elijah and kings of the eminence of David. It would have been easy, and almost certainly had been too easy, to rely heavily on the leadership offered by such figures. Most of all it is clear that reliance on the prestige of the kingship of the royal house of David had emerged as a hoped-for guarantee of Israel's safety and security (cf. the powerful expectations voiced in such a psalm as Psalm 2). Such hopes in a human institution, no matter how celebrated and prestigious, had been shown to be a dangerous illusion. So we find that subtly hidden behind the Deuteronomic portrait of Moses lie implicit warnings concerning the dangers of over much trust in human kingship. Ultimately the place accorded to Israel's kings in Deuteronomy is a surprisingly modest one, and certainly one that was careful to ensure that kings did not usurp the authority of Moses.

From a spiritual, rather than political, perspective this story of how God refused the request of Moses that he should enter the land is remarkably instructive. It presents the doctrine, with a rather mysterious matter-of-factness, that even the greatest and worthiest of leaders may suffer and experience punishment along with, and even on behalf of, those who are served. So the idea is born that the true

11

man of God will be a 'Suffering Servant', and will be embroiled in a deeply personal way with the pains and misfortunes of others for whom he seeks to win deliverance.

In a helpful and positive suggestion it appears probable that the remarkable portrait of the Suffering Servant of God in Isa. 53 may partly have been shaped by the tradition of Moses' denial of a place in the Promised Land. At the very least it is clear that the problem of why the innocent suffer *with* the guilty was beginning to be keenly felt by the time Deuteronomy was compiled. Nor could this hold short of raising awareness that the innocent may suffer *for* the guilty! The point is put with some force in 3. 26: *But because of you the Lord angrily brushed me aside and would not listen.* This goes further than simply pointing out that Moses was caught up in the wrongdoing of his fellow fugitives from slavery who refused to venture into the land. The point is a significant one and reflects one of the deepest and most enduring facets of the spiritual insights of the Old Testament. The notion of a shared reality of life as the people of God involves a depth of sharing which may include the pain and justifiable punishment of others. Biblical individualism recognizes that it has limitations and boundaries which arise from the fact that no individual human being is 'an island'. So with Moses a remarkable anticipation is made of the pathway to the Cross of Jesus Christ.

The God who speaks
4. 1–43

The dangers of idolatry
4. 1–8

The section comprising 4. 1–43, which we now encounter, stands as an interlude before the giving of God's covenant laws in Deut. 4. 44–46. It provides a preface to the Deuteronomic lawbook – a point which is reflected in REB's printing of a short break at this point. If, as scholars have suggested, the historical introduction of chapters 1–3 was added at a late stage – almost certainly when the law book of Deuteronomy was linked with the history contained in Joshua, Judges, I and II Samuel, I and II Kings – then 4. 1–40 offers a reflective interlude bringing to the surface a point of major emphasis. This concerns the nature of God and the danger of idolatry. It is most probably one of the very latest reflections and digressions to have been added to the book.

12

Once this temptation facing the book's first readers is recognized, it explains both the urgency of the warning and the emphasis attached to the assurance given in verses 29–31 that, even in exile, all hope will never be lost. There is even a slight note of tension between the sternness of the warnings about destruction and expulsion from the land given in verses 26–27, and the larger hope embraced in verse 31. The attentive reader should also consider 8. 21. Clearly the issue of Israel's future lay clouded in uncertainty. The insistence on the triumph of God's love for Israel when set against the nation's apostasy and the possibility of its complete disintegration present an unresolved tension.

The section begins in vv. 1–8 by introducing the central form and purpose of Deuteronomy as a book. The title *statutes and laws* (vv. 1–8; NRSV 'statutes and ordinances') is used to described its varied rulings (cf. also 4. 45). The term here translated 'law' particularly applied to rulings applicable to civil and criminal law. It is a distinctive feature of Deuteronomy that, by such terminology, it brings all such civil legislation under the broader umbrella of religious obligation (cf. below on v. 8). Accordingly specifically religious instructions also form a significant feature of the law book. The use of severe legal punishments to enforce religious conformity represents its most dangerous legacy (cf. 13. 1–18). The claim to the comprehensive and exclusive nature of the laws (4. 2) reflects similar formulations in other ancient law codes. The details of the specific rulings of the laws appear to have been drawn from records of individual cases which were recorded and then used to establish precedents for wider application. The immutability of what was laid down reflected the high level of authority accorded to it, without precluding that its interpretation could be further developed. If justice was to be granted to the entire nation then it had to be an 'equal justice'. The events that took place at the sanctuary of the god Baal at Baal-peor are recounted in Num. 25. 1–5 (v. 3).

That only a small part of the community who had escaped from the slavery of Egypt survived to enter the land (v. 4) was an important feature of the testing and judgement represented by the years spent in the wilderness (cf. on 2. 14–15). Nevertheless Deuteronomy repeatedly addresses the survivors as a large group who had been eyewitnesses of the earlier events from the time of the revelation on Mount Horeb.

Throughout the section the Deuteronomic author establishes the oneness of the present generation with faithful Israelites of the past by

13

skilful use of forms of direct address. Past temptations are clearly presented as continuing into the present, and the speeches of Moses bridge the intervals of time between those who had been delivered from Egypt, those who had stood on Mount Horeb and those who were about to cross into the land. To a significant degree this rather overlooks the claim that almost the entire generation that had stood at Mount Horeb had perished after their courage failed them when the report of the spies was presented. It is wholly in line with this sense of standing together before the word of God that we are made to feel that a new generation of Israel has arisen to form the readers for the law book. All hear directly, and for themselves, the word of God through Moses.

That the formulation of laws represents a form of wisdom (v. 6) reflects the broad understanding that wisdom was a desirable acquisition for every citizen who sought learning and insight. It brought mastery of life and its complexities. That Deuteronomy, as a written book of law, was influenced by the wisdom tradition, which is more typically represented in the book of Proverbs, reflects that wisdom was itself a widely diffused intellectual tradition seeking insight into the mastery of life. The directness of Israel's relationship with the LORD God (v. 7) was important, since it dispensed with the popular polytheistic belief in the need for intermediary deities who acted as go-betweens for the people and the Most High God. The emphasis upon the divine 'nearness' contrasts with the related, but contrasting, emphasis upon God's dwelling in heaven (cf. 26. 15).

The designation *all this code of laws* (v. 8; NRSV 'this entire law') describes the contents of Deuteronomy as 'law' (Heb. *torah*), which becomes a key term for the understanding of the Old Testament in both Jewish and Christian tradition. Its basic sense is 'direction, instruction', rather than 'statute' in the purely legal sense and it came to be used to describe the entire contents, not of Deuteronomy only, but of the first five books of the Old Testament (the Pentateuch). Legal statutes are included, but so also are more broadly directed instructions for religion and life.

The great temptation
4. 9–20

The greatest temptation that is presumed to face Israel is that of idolatry, and a new, and highly distinctive, argument to demonstrate the folly of this sin is presented in 4. 9–31. It represents one of the

14

longest warnings against idolatry to be found in the Old Testament, comparable to that of Isa. 44. 9–20. However, instead of focusing on the contention that an image can only be a humanly fashioned attempt to make a god, it argues from the report of God's self-revelation on Mount Horeb. So it draws extensive theological inferences from the earlier account in Exod. 19. 16–25 which describes the sights and sounds of what occurred there. No likeness of God could be seen, and so none can be made. To do so would falsify the understanding of God and would betray the truth that Israel had been entrusted with a true knowledge of God.

From a historical perspective there have been various attempts to unravel from the reports of God's revelation a more scientifically amenable interpretation of the event. Among the suggestions put forward is the claim that there was a volcanic eruption accounting for the emphasis upon fire and smoke. This, in turn, would have implications about the location of Mount Horeb (Sinai). Yet all of these attempts have proved fruitless and give rise to implausible geographical complexities. The biblical tradition simply reflects features of awesome natural phenomena, including violent thunderstorms, the smoke and flame of an altar fire, and possibly also, volcanic eruptions. They have been combined into one single episode to affirm the awesome, and unapproachable, nature of God. The lack of any visible form of God (v. 12) was important and is in accord with the tradition of Exod. 33. 18–23 that the presence of God can never be seen by human eyes. Similar restraint concerning God's unseen form is found in prophetic visions. Cf. Isa. 6. 1–3; Ezek. 1. 22–25. The prophet only sees the heavenly throne of God and the surrounding heavenly servants, in an inner vision; the actual form of God remains hidden and unyielding to human description.

The term 'covenant' (4. 13) to describe the relationship between Israel and the LORD God is a key one, since it came ultimately to be used to describe the entire Hebrew Bible as the literature of God's 'covenant' (= Latin *Testamentum*; Eng. Testament). The term is employed to describe human agreements between individuals, as well as international treaties in which specific terms and penalties for default could be included. In all such agreements it was usual for a deity, or the several deities of the respective parties, to oversee the enforcement of what was agreed. It seems highly probable that Deuteronomy has drawn extensively on familiarity with the forms and conventions which were employed in such international treaties where elaborate documentation was commonplace. Thereafter it is the usage of the idea of covenant in Deuteronomy which strongly characterizes its wider biblical development.

The specific reference to the *Ten Commandments* (v. 13 literally 'Ten Words') is amplified by their being listed in 5. 6–21.

The Second Commandment (5. 8) prohibits the use of images in the worship of the LORD God, so the introduction of a reason for this prohibition was felt to be in order (vv. 15–20). The basic argument is that such images would be misleading representations of God and would entice the worshipper into a false understanding of the relationship between God and humankind. God always remains the initiator and author of such a relationship, whereas an image may lead the worshipper into believing that he, or she, has power to control, and even use, God to serve a human purpose. The exposition here is a fuller, and undoubtedly later, exploration of that prohibition and extends it to cover the use of any visual image or representation of human or animal forms of any kind. It is then extended yet further to include symbols of the heavenly bodies, as the sun, moon and stars (v. 19).

By extending the prohibition in this way the exposition moves into far wider areas of religious symbolism, which have, in historical experience, led to violent reactions in religion against the use of any form of visual symbolic indication of divine power and presence, and even, at times, to the repudiation of all visual art forms (iconoclasm).

The folly of making images
  4. 21–31

The folly of making images in any form is then further interpreted as the supreme manifestation of Israel's disloyalty to the covenant. To what extent there had been a widespread use of such images, set up in Israel's major sanctuaries, as reported of the bull-calf images in Bethel and Dan (cf. I Kgs. 12. 28–30) has been widely discussed. Were they understood to be 'images' of the LORD God, or merely pedestals which symbolized the divine presence? The extent to which the cherubim set up in the Jerusalem temple might also have been interpreted as 'images' of heavenly beings has also called for careful examination. Clearly the Deuteronomic movement sought to enforce a more rigid interpretation of the Second Commandment than had previously been current (cf. also II Kgs. 18. 4). The simplest and most popular form of an image of a god was one carved from wood (cf. 4. 23), but often covered with a thin sheathing of precious metal, either of silver or gold. Larger images set up in a sanctuary were usually carved from stone. More durable and substantial images were cast in a mould, again preferably using precious metals, as in the case of the narrative concerning the cast image of the Golden Calf (Exod. 32. 1–35). The use of images of any kind was covered by this prohibition, and the understanding is that they would provide a form of immediate, guaranteed, access to God. Among the many popular forms of such images, which archaeological excavation has brought to light, were small effigies of a pregnant woman, presumably a goddess (Ishtar-Astarte?). These appear to have been private possessions and were little more than amulets ('lucky charms'), to help in securing safe (and healthy) childbirth.

The forewarning of exile among the nations in 4. 27, declaring this to be God's appointed mode of punishment for those who had been disloyal through the use of images, brings out one of the most deeply felt concerns of the Deuteronomic authors. Evidently such removal into exile had already overtaken many in the nation and this early forewarning of it served as an explanation for such a cruel fate.

The denigratory rejection of the use of images, ridiculing their powerlessness (4. 28 cf. Isa. 44. 18–20), recognizes the temptation that, in a foreign land, the temptation would be all the greater to follow the example of non-Jewish neighbours. The assurance of v. 29 – . . . *if it is with all your heart and soul that you search* . . . – finds a close parallel in Jer. 29. 12–13. It brings out the inwardness of the obedience that Deuteronomy strove to encourage. This was not to be one of outward conformity alone, but was to spring from a true heart-searching examination of motives and desires. The overall importance of the promise as an assurance that life among the nations would not mean a separation from God cannot be overrated. God would never completely hide from the people – even when they were carried off into distant lands of exile. It has given rise to the fundamental characteristic of Jewish life among the nations in putting prayer and an inward spirit of self-examination above mere concern with holy places. The 'turning back' to God is to be an inward act of personal penitence.

The true knowledge of God
   4. 32–40

In contrast to the false attempts by human beings to make images of God, the only true knowledge was to be found when God spoke from

17

Mount Horeb to Moses. The claim that the people heard God's voice reflects their hearing of the thunder (Exod. 19. 18–19), but only Moses communed with God (Exod. 24. 18; 31. 18). The proof of God's existence is to be found in the word that has been given through Moses (4. 35–36) not in the fashioning of images which may purport to look like God, but cannot in reality do so, since God's appearance is unknown. Revelation must come from God to humankind. It cannot come from human attempts to make a look-alike god, which will only mislead. Verses 39–40 then proceed to present the most outright affirmation of the entire book that there is only one God and no other exists (monotheism). The wording of 6. 4 is less decisive in that it does not explicitly deny the existence of other gods.

Cities set aside for legal jurisdiction
4. 41–43

The brief note regarding the allocation of three cities on the eastern side of the River Jordan is introduced at this point in order to complete the record of arrangements made there. Their purpose is explained more fully in Deut. 19. 1–15 and they are mentioned at this early point because of their location. Their purpose was to provide a protected basis for public investigation of charges of murder before any punishment was carried out. This would easily occur through hasty attempts to secure revenge for a death, however caused. In noting the appointment of these cities in Transjordan, even before the introduction of the law code which explains how they are to operate, we see Deuteronomy's anxiety to give a high priority to its large territorial claims.

Preface to the covenant laws
4. 44–11. 32

The law code of Deuteronomy properly begins in chapter 12 with provision for the setting up of an altar at the place which God will choose. It extends as far as 26. 19. It is, however, given an extended introduction, beginning in 4. 44, which includes the listing of the Ten Commandments as the primary rules, or terms, of God's covenant with Israel. Alongside these commandments we have a series of speeches given by Moses on their great importance for the welfare and survival of the nation. These admonitions are interspersed with

18

warnings of the temptations that will exist for Israel to neglect and disobey them. In many of their features these admonitions and warnings represent the heartland of biblical spirituality, exploring the inner thoughts and feelings which are to govern worship, or which may lead to its neglect. The relationship between the commandments and the law code of 12. 1–26. 19 is an important one, since, in spite of appearances, they do not represent two different collections, or classes, of law. The commandments provide the broad headings and principles of conduct, and the laws fill out these principles by showing how they must be applied in society.

The law of the covenant
4. 44–5. 5

Deuteronomy is first and foremost a book of law (*torah*; cf. note on 4. 8), and to record the content of this law is its central purpose. But it is law of a distinctive kind and possessed of a special authority which derives from the time at which it was given and the person (Moses) through whom it was mediated to Israel. So, although the repetition of the occasion of their being declared to Israel in 4. 46–49 appears superfluous, it makes their claim on Israel unmistakably clear. The terms used in 4. 45 to describe three types of legal, or official, ruling, were originally applicable in different contexts, but with some potential overlap. Deuteronomy's bringing all three classes of ruling together and designating them collectively as 'a code of laws' (Heb. *torah*) marks an important step in the formation of the Hebrew biblical canon since this is the title that has ultimately been extended in meaning to cover the entire Pentateuch. By linking this to the occasion of their original declaration to Israel their superior claim over other forms of legislation is established. No subsequent royal decree, or prophetic revelation, could displace them, or rob them of the priority which they claimed. The law that was given with the birth of the nation becomes its birthright, without which the nation cannot continue.

The claim to territorial possessions on the east of the River Jordan (4. 46–49) remained an important, if largely ideal, claim to territory which had early fallen victim to its exposure to other claimants. The Jordan valley represented a lucrative trade route between several great civilizations (Mesopotamia, Phoenicia, Egypt and Africa). It also formed a significant barrier which left the tribes settled to the east of it cut off from the major part of Israel.

19

The Deuteronomic insistence that Moses addressed *all Israel* (5. 1) and that the entire nation was present for the giving of the Commandments reflects the three major realities which Deuteronomy upholds: one nation, one land, one law. Mount Horeb (Sinai) was the birthplace of Israel as a nation, and so the law given at that time (5. 2–5) remained forever an inescapable privilege and obligation upon every member of it. The covenant made then was the covenant which constituted Israel as a nation (cf. Exod. 19. 5–6). The later reference to a further covenant made in the plains of Moab, before the crossing of the River Jordan, was not another (i.e. different) covenant (Deut. 29. 1), but a renewal and reaffirmation of this primary covenant made on Mount Horeb. Moses was the one and only mediator of this covenant for Israel (5. 5). We should compare this assertion with Exod. 24. 9–14 which describes how Moses went up the mountain accompanied by Aaron, Nadab, Abihu and seventy of the elders of Israel who 'saw' the God of Israel and ate a meal there.

The Ten Commandments
5. 6–21

Since the Ten Commandments have been one of the most widely known features of the Old Testament they have understandably been subjected to intense scrutiny. This applies both to their moral demands and literary form. The questions concerning their setting and literary form may be considered first. The listing of the Ten Commandments has already been made earlier in Exod. 20. 2–17 so that their repetititon here is unexpected and gives extra emphasis to them. The act of repetition marks them out as standing apart from other biblical lists of laws. The wording in the two contexts is slightly varied, chiefly because Exod. 20 gives additional reasons for observing the sabbath. However the strikingly significant feature is that Exod. 20 sets out the contents of the tablets which were said to have been smashed by Moses according to Exod. 32. When they are redrafted in Exod. 34 their contents differ yet again (cf. Deut. 10. 4–5). The conclusion that has been drawn by many scholars is that it was only at a late stage of the growth of the narrative of Genesis–Deuteronomy that the premature introduction of the Ten Commandments into the text of Exod. 20 took place. (The question is examined in more detail in my commentary in *New Interpreter's Bible*, Vol. 2, pp. 325–37). So the formulation of the commandments in Deut 5. 6–21 represents their earliest written recording and the earlier anticipation of this in Exod. 20 has been made on account of their importance to the Mosaic (Sinai) covenant.

Form The form of the Ten Commandments as the direct speech of God is remarkable, since elsewhere it is only prophets who presume to speak in this fashion. This speech-form lends to the commandments a unique level of authority. The numbering of them has been understood differently in different traditions, with Roman Catholics and Martin Luther following Jewish tradition in regarding the prologue (v. 6) as the first commandment and taking vv. 7–10 to form the second of them. The Reformed tradition has followed Calvin in regarding v. 7 as the first commandment and vv. 8–10 as the second, prohibiting idolatry.

The form of eight of the commandments is that of categorical prohibitions, precluding certain actions and attitudes. Contrastingly the fourth (sabbath) and fifth commandments (honouring parents) are formulated positively. The suggestion has at times been widely canvassed among scholars that these too must originally have been set out as prohibitions. This would have allowed all of them to be very short formulations, easily inscribed on a stone tablet. Yet this conclusion appears both unnecessary and unlikely. It is the subject of the action commanded that dictates the form used, whether a prohibition or a positive injunction to act in a particular way.

The fact that the commandments lack any threat or prescription of punishment, as laws in the normal sense require, has led to suggestions that there is an implied punishment (excommunication from the community or perhaps even a sentence of death?). Yet neither of these conclusions is either probable or necessary.

The fact is noteworthy, however, that several of the commandments deal with offences covered elsewhere by more formal legislation (e.g. murder, theft and adultery). Clearly the Ten Commandments are meant to stand alongside, rather than to replace, normal legal activities.

Content In the matters they deal with the Ten Commandments represent a form of fundamental ethical and spiritual direction. How then are we to interpret the significance of their highly distinctive form? Following a widely adopted suggestion scholars have sought to understand the commandments as a form of basic law, or covenant law, or even criminal law (scholars have noted that several of the commandments deal with matters which relate to potential capital

21

offences). Yet all these suggestions inevitably narrow the range of their meaning and ignore the markedly educational purpose which they display. They have been compared to fundamental human rights, or have been regarded as exemplary of basic ethical principles ('fundamental ethic'). It is these latter suggestions that come closest to allowing full scope to the broad range of issues with which they deal. They aim to cover a very wide range of human spiritual and moral concerns, making them into fundamental 'rules of life'. This approximates closely to the way they have been understood in the Christian tradition, which has tended to distinguish between the moral laws (Ten Commandments) and the ritual (or ceremonial) laws of the Old Testament. More recently scholars have drawn attention to the way in which they provide thematic headings for the sequence of issues dealt with in greater detail in chapters 12–26. We may examine them in detail in the following manner:

5. 6   *Prologue: I am the LORD your God.* This prologue to the commandments almost certainly reflects the liturgical setting in which they were once read out. Although Jewish interpretation, followed by the Christian Catholic and Lutheran traditions, sees in it the first commandment, it implies a less than universal applicability of the commandments which follow. The declaration *I am the LORD your God* is typically Deuteronomic in its formulation and implies a two-sided covenant obligation, raising the understanding that these commandments are 'covenant law'.

5. 7   *First commandment: You must have no other gods beside me.* The NRSV translation reads 'before me' and the different renderings (cf. also the NRSV margin) point to a long-standing difficulty since the Hebrew preposition 'beside' can also mean 'before', and even 'in preference to'. The commandment precludes worshipping other gods, or goddesses, alongside the LORD. Most ancient Near Eastern deities were thought to be arranged in a pantheon with one 'High God' at the top, and other gods and goddesses surrounding him in the manner of a human household. There is substantial evidence that a goddess figure (Anat, Ishtar) was sometimes revered alongside the LORD. However this practice did not receive official approval in the major Israelite temples in Bethel and Jerusalem. It appears that local variations about the relationships between gods and goddesses in the many sanctuary traditions abounded. The commandments sought to establish a coherent and consistent presentation of Israel's sole

God. Difficulties arose because of popular attempts to formulate recognizable relationships between the gods of different shrines and the temptation to adapt Israelite worship to widely known (Canaanite) traditions.

Overall popular religion in the ancient world was many-sided and customarily focused on a number of gods with one of their number being celebrated as supreme 'King', or 'Father', of them (cf. Ps. 95. 3). What is distinctive about the Israelite faith, as Deuteronomy interprets it, is its strong note of exclusivity. Yet this commandment, in the strict sense, falls short of a rigid monotheism since it allows the understanding that there may be other deities beside the LORD God, who are worshipped by other nations. It is these that are to have no place in Israel's faith, and the issue is not altogether consistently presented in Deuteronomy. However this commandment came to be widely understood by Jews and Christians in this strictly monotheistic sense with a firm denial that any other gods exist at all, except in the imagination of human minds.

5. 8–10 *Second commandment: You are not to make a carved image for yourself.* The inference is that it would be an image, or symbolic representation, of the LORD God of Israel, since worship of other gods has already been ruled out. It is evident that symbolic images and representations played a major role in all ancient religions and at one time did so in ancient Israel. So the sacred serpent which Moses upheld was once approved, but subsequently rejected (Num. 21. 6–9; cf. II Kgs. 18. 4). Contrastingly the cherubim of the Jerusalem temple retained approval (I Kgs. 6. 23–28). In much starker contrast the bullcalf images of the sanctuaries at Bethel and Dan were roundly condemned (I Kgs. 12. 25–32, as is Aaron's notorious Golden Calf in Exod. 32. 1–35). The interested reader can also consider carefully the prophet Ezekiel's reproof of what he knew to exist in the Jerusalem temple (cf. Ezek. 8. 1–18). How the various differences were understood and justified is not altogether clear. Overall the idea was rejected that a human being could have a 'god in the pocket' (i.e. could manipulate divine power) by fashioning an image which in some sense represented the deity and dispensed power.

5. 11 *Third commandment: You shall not make wrong use of the name of the LORD your God.* The REB translation endeavours to bring out the comprehensive nature of what is prohibited. This includes invoking God's name to swear an oath in support of what is false, using

23

God's name to back up magical incantations and the like, besides the more familiar interpretation of using the name wantonly, or blasphemously. Early interpretations focused chiefly on prohibiting the application of the divine name to an idol, or to an unworthy creature, hence linking it with the preceding commandment.

5. 12–15   *Fourth commandment: Observe the sabbath day and keep it holy.* The addition of verses 13–15 make this the longest commandment, and it is amplified slightly differently in the parallel text in Exod. 20. 8–11. The careful justification of the demand recognizes that it was difficult to enforce and could be easily set aside for selfish reasons (cf. Amos 8. 5; Neh. 13. 15–22). It is highly unlikely that it was ever commonplace for the community (or priests) to treat a breach of the sabbath commandment as a capital offence (as described in Num. 15. 32–36). The priority of emphasis in Deuteronomy is on the human need for physical and mental rest. The origins of the observance lie further back in the marking of divisions in the lunar month into days appropriate for worship.

Jesus' relaxed attitude to the demand (cf. Luke 6. 1–5) and opposition to any rigid enforcement of punitive measures for breaches of it, almost certainly represents an attitude already current in Jewish life. Even Nehemiah could do no more than hinder trading on the sabbath!

In Christian tradition the widened understanding of the Ten Commandments as expressions of universal law for all humankind, and not simply Jewish law, eventually found difficulty with the sabbath. Since the Church had adopted Sunday as 'The Lord's Day' when public worship was conducted (cf. Rev. 1. 10), the question of observance of the sabbath was set in a fresh perspective. With the renewed focus on the Ten Commandments after the Reformation this gave rise in some branches of the Christian Reformed tradition to a concern to reinstate Christian observance of a seventh-day sabbath (e.g. Seventh Day Adventists). More widely it has frequently led to a concern to regard 'the Lord's Day' (Sunday) as a Christian sabbath and to impose strict rules and guidelines on what activities may be appropriate. Such guidelines can become needlessly irksome, but quite clearly the fundamental principle of the human need for a time of withdrawal from normal work activities is of profound importance.

5. 16   *Fifth commandment: Honour your father and your mother.* The commandment focuses on recognition of the primary role played

24

by the family in the structure and economic health of society. Problems arose when the inevitable process of ageing and failing health meant that senior members of a household could no longer work. So the commandment has a strong economic relevance since it insists that members of the community were not to be dishonoured and humiliated when they ceased to contribute to the family's workforce. Clearly, however, there is also present in the commandment an awareness of the importance of respect, honour and integrity within a household. Throughout the Old Testament shame is regarded as a destructive force which is to be avoided in the maintenance of relationships. Respect for the experience and wisdom of older members of the household was of paramount importance. Since Deuteronomy stresses the primary role of parents in moral education (cf. 6. 7), the upholding of parental authority was a contributory factor in promoting this.

5. 17 *Sixth commandment: Do not commit murder.* The NRSV margin reads 'kill' instead of 'murder' which recognizes the fact that the Hebrew word used is a distinctive one, and not the more familiar verb used for 'killing, putting to death' generally. Deuteronomy's laws provided for capital punishment in appropriate circumstances (cf. 19. 11–13), besides recognizing the inevitability of killing in warfare (cf. 20. 10–18). It therefore becomes evident that this commandment is directed against forms of unlawful killing. Even the translation 'murder' conveys a narrower significance than that which is intended. In the forefront is the concern to outlaw the practice of vengeance killing which must have remained a deeply embedded feature of Israelite life, as it was in many ancient (and modern!) communities. All too often feuding between families, even resulting from cases of accidental deaths, were avenged by a member of the victim's family. Popular convention conceded that there existed a 'right' to exact such retribution. Accordingly it is likely that frequently no punitive action was taken when a vengeance killing occurred without recourse to any public investigation or trial (cf. more recent lynchings!).

It is likely, however, that the commandment was aimed at prohibiting all forms of unlawful killing in which no opportunity for a fair trial was given. The killing of an intruder unnecessarily (cf. Exod. 22. 4) or any act of needless disregard for the safety and protection of human life was outlawed by this commandment. The modern preference for the translation 'murder' only partly alleviates this lack of precise definition. Since the Old Testament allows capital punishment in appropriate circumstances and contains carefully framed laws dealing with murder and accidental manslaughter the main focus here must rest on cases of unlawful killing where such laws were proving to be limited in their effectiveness.

5. 18   *Seventh commandment: Do not commit adultery.* The prohibition is aimed at securing the integrity of family life and ensuring a husband's right to the paternity of his children who would become a part of his household. The rigid sexual restraints and laws contained in Deuteronomy show clearly the seemingly never ending range of problems which human sexuality has generated for society. Hos. 2. 4 (cf. Jer. 3. 8) suggests that an adulterous woman would be divorced, but Deut. 22. 2 demands the death penalty for such an offence. Strong feelings of solidarity in an extended family provided the basic framework of economic, social and religious obligations which lay at the heart of moral restraints for each person.

Marriage and parenthood therefore called for special care and protection in Israel's legal system. This need was all the more acutely felt in a context where polygamy was tolerated and brought the further complexities of rivalry between wives and competition to secure favours for particular children. The terms in which divorce and remarriage were acceptable, and the rights directed towards upholding the status of a wife chosen from among prisoners of war, and of children of rival wives, are spelt out in greater detail in the law code (cf. Deut. 21. 10–17). Laws dealing with cases of rape and adultery were also harsh and brutal, but also incidentally reveal an awareness that evidence of a woman's deliberate misconduct might be difficult to prove (cf. 22. 25–27). This helps to explain the need for the commandment here and the retention of the ominously archaic provisions for a jealous husband preserved in Num. 5. 13–31. The problems and attendant dangers of popular suspicion and difficulties in proving sexual misconduct provide the point of the poetic wisdom saying of Prov. 30. 18–19.

5. 19   *Eighth commandment: Do not steal.* The misappropriation of another's property posed significant difficulties for ancient Israel's legal system to deal with. This was not the consequence of any failure to perceive the wrongfulness of such actions, nor out of disregard for an individual to hold personal possessions. Rather such problems arose because proof of ownership might often be difficult to establish (cf. Exod. 22. 10–15). The written recording of business deals, with

very complex and formal terms of agreement, backed up by the use of oaths, seals and witnesses to validate transactions are all reflections of this.

Clearly problems of stealing from flocks and herds, as well as the occasional need to leave property in another's care, could all add to the difficulties of establishing satisfactory proof of ownership. In the case of otherwise unresolvable disputes over such matters the local priest could be brought in to adjudicate, showing that it was important to reach some final decision, even if it were no more than the imposition of an oath whereby accusations and suspicions could be laid to rest.

5. 20 *Ninth commandment: Do not give baseless evidence against your neighbour.* The problem posed by malicious accusations in a trial proceeding could be dangerous and deeply disruptive of community life, even resulting in the death of an innocent person and the misappropriation of his land (cf. I Kgs. 21. 1–14). Although formal legal charges are primarily in mind wider abuse through slanderous accusations is not to be ruled out (cf. Exod. 23. 1). It is noteworthy that the rulings in Deuteronomy concerning accusations of wrongful worship needed to be carefully safeguarded by special warnings on this point (cf. 17. 2–7).

5. 21 *Tenth commandment: Do not lust after your neighbour's wife.* The NRSV more faithfully represents the Hebrew with its 'Neither shall you covet your neighbour's wife'. Although REB's rendering may be a legitimate inference, the prohibition is not against lust directly, but against seeking to entice another man's wife to enter one's own household (cf. I Sam. 25. 2–42). The fact that desiring, and wanting to obtain possession of, another man's wife is placed ahead of coveting other property has led many scholars to conclude that the original commandment focused exclusively on such action and was only later extended to cover other property. It was not simply adultery with another's wife that was outlawed, which is already covered by the seventh commandment, but participation in any serious attempt to seduce and entice the wife of another person in a social context which allowed quite readily for divorce and polygamy.

The whole question of 'coveting' in this tenth commandment has raised much discussion, largely on account of its condemning an attitude and mindset, rather than an overt action. This in turn has encouraged many scholars to interpret the coveting as implying an

27

active taking of steps to satisfy one's desire. This rather strained interpretation has arisen out of a belief that the Ten Commandments were very specific and legalistically oriented (a bad attitude of mind can scarcely be punished!), rather than condemnatory of inward desiring. Yet the contemporary Israelite teaching of wisdom places great stress on the need to encourage positive and heart-searching attitudes of mind. Clearly the instability of households in which the women members might be easily enticed away was wholly undesirable, and the necessity of removing any risk of such instability was a matter of great importance. Accordingly the inclusion of this comprehensive commandment sought to protect marriage and the right to hold property with reasonable security.

After the great popularity in the Medieval and Reformation periods of Christian use of the Ten Commandments as a primary focus of religious and moral education, interest in them waned significantly during the nineteenth and twentieth centuries. The Victorian poet A. H. Clough's satirical poem *A New Decalogue* is a good illustration of the misapprehensions about them which have encouraged this. There emerged a popular belief that, taken as absolute principles, they are unworkable and are in any case formulated too negatively. Consequently they leave too many loopholes for evasion. In related fashion post-Enlightenment interest in moral issues urged the view that the pursuit of virtue requires initiative and effort, rather than simply refraining from active wrongdoing. Although the issue requires to be carefully considered, it is clear that the formulation of the commandments was never intended to circumscribe the limits of personal responsibility, nor to ignore the wider concerns with community solidarity and shared obligations. Much of their force has rested on their focus on individual personal commitment in situations where there was no effective police authority and very little confidence could be set on the public administration of law.

As their setting in Deuteronomy shows, the Ten Commandments were directed towards establishing broad guidelines and fundamental attitudes which required to be more fully amplified by reference to the provisions of the law. At their best they served as directives to establish major areas where right conduct has to be observed and respected. Even biblical scholars have at times been mistaken in supposing them to represent a separate kind of law which stood apart from more familiar and formal legal procedures. Certainly they looked to the proper application of judicial processes, whenever these were trustworthy and in place. All too often, however, both Jews (and later Christians) have had to live in situations where no police force existed and the public representatives of justice (sometimes acting under foreign officials) were unreliable, often untrustworthy, and sometimes actively hostile.

As they have been received by Jews and Christians the commandments represent a very comprehensive code of behaviour regarding personal conduct and attitude. They draw attention to matters of religious and social conduct where the law may prove to be weak (as in a refusal to take action against a traditional 'avenger of blood'), or unable, for lack of reliable evidence, to act with decisive effect (e.g. over cases of perjury, adultery, theft, etc.). They show that morality does not begin and end with observance of the law but covers a much wider area of life and educational nurture. It is precisely this point which Jesus reinforces and extends by regarding the command to love one's neighbour as comprehending a whole range of more detailed, and unspecified, social demands.

Divine authority and the divine mediator
5. 22–33

Deuteronomy's account of the giving of the Ten Commandments to Israel through Moses concludes with a description of the manifestation of God at that time. In the biblical narrative two issues are highlighted: first the overwhelming demonstration of God's majesty which shows that it truly is God who lends authority to the commandments. This in turn explains the necessity for the role of Moses to be the mediator between God and the people. Left to themselves the people could not bear the encounter with God's presence. To do so would have overwhelmed and destroyed them (v. 25). Pushed to its inevitable conclusion, however, this recognition would imply that there can be no communication between human beings and their Creator. Yet this is not the case; such communication is both possible and has become a reality since God's chosen mediator – Moses – stands between them. Without this mediation the very glory of God would make revelation impossible.

Two vital biblical truths are brought together here in a striking fashion. God is altogether greater and more awe-inspiring than even the most lavish expressions of human language can describe – God is at once both a cloak of impenetrable darkness and a fire of unbearable intensity and brightness. This majestic presence can, however, be revealed on earth through the words of a human mediator. The

29

unknowable is made known since, although human beings may not penetrate to see the heavenly world, God may nevertheless reach out to touch a human life and thereby make known the divine will for humankind.

A further remarkable feature of this revelation of God on Mount Horeb is that it brings together three aspects of the divine–human encounter. First and foremost Israel is made aware of God through the laws of the covenant. Revelation is not about God's mysterious 'essence', but about the divine relationship to human beings. For human beings to live together in community imposes rules and obligations upon them if the full created and creative potential of human life is to be enjoyed. Yet even this awareness of life's duties and demands would remain meaningless without a leader and guide whose task is to explain the nature of these demands and show how people may respond to them. This is what Moses achieves through the provision of the written commandments. Experience of life itself plunges every person into situations which call for right choices and responses, if the world is not to relapse into chaos. The laws given through Moses show how these choices and responses are to be made.

Nevertheless, there exists behind these experiences and these laws a greater hidden reality which cannot be fully grasped by the human mind. Even in revealing God, the Bible constantly reminds us that such revelation only partly lifts the curtain of mystery which hides the fullness of God's Being from human eyes. All human knowledge of the divine world must never lose awareness of where the mystery begins. It is appropriate therefore to note the emphasis which is placed here on the report that God speaks 'out of darkness' (v. 24). Nor is the sense of wavering human loyalty and a reluctance to obey the divine commands left out in the wistful 'Would that they may always be of a mind to fear me' (v. 29). God always wants for us a better life than we want for ourselves!

Learning to love God
   6. 1–19

This is probably the most familiar and widely cited chapter in the entire book, and its force lies in its concern to place knowledge of, and respect for, the Ten Commandments at the centre of life. It matches the importance of what is to be taught with a concern for actions and techniques showing how this is to be achieved. Accordingly the central theme is presented with forcefulness and rhetorical imagina-

30

tion. This shows already in the opening words in which Moses assumes his full authority as the covenant mediator between God and Israel – *which the* LORD *your God commanded* me *to teach* you. Noteworthy also are the promises attached to the keeping of the commandments – *that you may enjoy long life* (v. 2) – *you will prosper and increase greatly* (v. 3).

The linking of rewards in the form of a long life and prosperity for obedience to God's law marks a distinctive feature of Deuteronomic teaching (6. 3). That it represents a relative, rather than an absolute, truth, is highly significant, and led to much fuller reflection on the problem of undeserved evil in the later books of Job and Ecclesiastes. It does, nonetheless, mark an important starting-point for reflection, since it is impossible to suppose that no connection at all exists between the moral health of society and its material prosperity and well-being.

The LORD *is our God, the* LORD *our one God* (6. 4) marks a central affirmation of faith, but one that has occasioned difficulty for modern translators, as the several alternative renderings in the margin of NRSV show. The traditional understanding has been that this is a straightforward doctrine of monotheism and that there is, and can be, only one God. Yet this is not precisely what is said, since the verse simply affirms that the LORD is 'one God'.

Read in the light of ancient religion more generally, what is primarily affirmed is that there is only one God for Israel (i.e. there are not different forms, or manifestations, of the LORD God at different sanctuaries); nor can the LORD be worshipped as one God (albeit the highest) among many (i.e. a family, or group, of gods) even at one great sanctuary. Both these ideas of the divine world were popularly current in antiquity as the Bible shows by its reference to many 'Baals' (i.e. local forms of Baal) and the prevalent portrayal of a pantheon of gods in which a divine family, or court (modelled on human royal courts), formed the focus of worship. This might include wives, sisters, sons, slaves, and the like, and encouraged ideas of intermediary beings who could be approached to intercede with the chief 'Most High' God. All such beliefs are excluded by Deuteronomy's insistence on the oneness of God. The book of Deuteronomy is not consistent about altogether denying the existence of other deities besides the LORD (cf. on 4. 35). For all major purposes, it insists that the LORD alone directs and rules both heaven and earth. Some scholars have found it helpful to describe this as 'practical monotheism'.

The command to love God (6. 5) has called for much discussion on

31

the grounds that it is a love that is commanded. The emphases upon divine wrath and anger which are strongly present in Deuteronomy, present a picture of a deity who often appears as a distant and unyielding heavenly disciplinarian. Yet overall there is a consistent concern to point to the loving, compassionate and life-affirming nature of God, which demands that those who worship should do so with a warmth and joy that recognizes a loving Father-God who is always more generous in giving than in receiving. Learning to love God becomes a prominent goal of worship and a primary educational aspect of its purpose.

Much discussion has arisen around the highly distinctive nature of the demand: 'You shall love the LORD your God'. Can such a love simply be commanded? This is especially relevant when so much weight is placed on the truths that God is wholly mysterious and has unlimited and irresistible power. Divine wrath is greatly to be feared (cf. 5. 22–7).

Love, however, does not exclude awe and must itself be subject to a process of education and learning. God's laws should become the occasion of great happiness and rejoicing, as Ps. 119 affirms. So a growing awareness of God, and the knowledge that this brings, should develop into a deepening love. Faith is a path to happiness, even though many obstacles may make that path difficult to follow. The command to love God therefore has provided faith with its ultimate goal, since learning to love God with a whole heart and mind points us to the deepest and truest fulfilment of human life. Only when that love is in place do we become what we truly are – children of God. Until we love God we shall always feel dissatisfied with life.

How Israel is to make sure that knowledge of the commandments is carried forward from one generation to the next is set out as a programme for remembering and reflection in all areas of daily life (6. 6–9). Each home is to be a school of learning in which the commandments are regularly taught and every practical avenue for encouraging and maintaining a knowledge of them is to be employed. The latter instruction has been widely taken literally in Jewish tradition, rather than metaphorically (i.e. 'keep thinking about them') by the provision of phylacteries. These are small boxes containing the text of Exod. 13. 1–10, 11–16 and Deut. 6. 4–9; 11. 13–21. They have assumed added importance in Judaism in displacing the wearing of amulets and other tokens as 'lucky charms'.

The message of vv. 10–15 serves as a warning against complacency since the land of Israel is described as already occupied and extensively developed with cities and towns. This is undoubtedly a picture confirmed by archaeological researches which have shown the rich growth in the civilization and development of the region over a long period. Overall, as in many comparable historical movements of conquest, the extent to which whole populations were expelled and others brought in to take their place has been greatly exaggerated by Deuteronomy and the accounts in the book of Joshua which it has influenced. In the book this taking over of the property of others is seen as a religious privilege, rather than a moral problem, and has evidently been directed towards encouraging Israel not to forfeit this land by turning away from God.

Deuteronomy's repeated insistence that the LORD alone is to be worshipped (6. 14–15) reveals, even unwittingly, how very mixed, and confused the actual religious life of the land of Israel had been. The Deuteronomic authors regard this variety of religious allegiance, which was for the most part widely tolerated, as a dangerous feature which ought to have been more firmly opposed than it clearly had been. One of the greatest issues that is raised by the book lies in its concern to suppress any form of tolerance in the interests of a firm and unyielding religious correctness. In retrospect it has sadly been the case that this emphasis on religious intolerance has been one of its strongest legacies.

The putting God *to the test* (6. 16) must here mean acting in a disloyal way to see if God would really punish such conduct. It may include flagrant acts of blasphemy to see whether God does act to uphold the holiness of the divine name. The 'testing' at Massah is recounted in Exod. 17. 7 (cf. Ps. 95. 8–9).

The concluding assertion that victory in battle will come as a consequence of religious loyalty in matters of conduct (6. 19) is a recurrent theme in Deuteronomy. As in its condemnation of Israel's idolatry, it represents a demand which unwittingly reflects a deep awareness on the part of the authors that Israel had shown itself, from a military perspective, to be weak and vulnerable. In coming to terms with this fact, which events had shown were lamentably true, they look for a spiritual, rather than a military renewal.

The meaning of the laws
  6. 20–25

The employment of a question and answer formula marks a distinctive feature of present day Jewish Passover ritual in which worship and respect for the divine law are brought together. The question *'What is the meaning of . . .?'* carries the sense of asking why observance of the law is such an important issue for every Jewish person. The form of reply in vv. 21–23 recounts the centrality of the story of the exodus as marking the moment when the unique bond between God and people was established. The insistence *it will be for our own good at all times* (6. 24) reflects yet again the strong Deuteronomic belief that obedience to God's law will provide a way of life which will be rewarded by prosperity and personal fulfilment for each individual.

The issue gives cause for serious and deep reflection in this regard. The broad assurance 'Keep the commandments . . . so that you may enjoy long life' (6. 1–3) strongly suggests that religion and morality will, in the final analysis, be simply a matter of self-interest. In its turn it then inevitably raises the question on the lips of victims of disease, poverty and tragic accidents 'Why me?' 'Have I been less devout or less conscientious than others?' In general Deuteronomy errs on the side of promising too much in the way of a prosperous and healthy life for those who keep God's commandments. The book is confident that people get what they deserve, and this is how it has been widely understood, even though this cannot be regarded as consistently true to human experience.

However, before dismissing this repeated Deuteronomic affirmation as less than true to life, and unchristian in that it leaves no place for the Cross of Jesus, we need to reflect on its more positive side. It does assert a relative truth since, in a broad perspective, we can accept that God's way as revealed in the commandments, precisely because it is the way of the Creator, is aimed at promoting fullness of human life, with all that this implies for health, happiness and prosperity. That there are limits to this in our individual experience must be tempered by recognizing that Deuteronomy emerged in a society in which the shared destiny of whole communities and nations was more prominent than a concern with the fate of individuals. The issue begins to be raised more fully in Deuteronomy in regard to the fate of Moses (see on 1. 37; 32. 51–52).

Moreover we learn from the prophets Jeremiah and Ezekiel (Jer. 31. 27–30; Ezek. 18. 1–32) that the first readers to whom Deuteronomy was addressed were strongly inclined to lay the blame for their misfortunes on their ancestors. Such led ultimately to an attitude of despair and inaction. It was important therefore, when deep political and social turmoil were being felt, that this doctrine of despair should be countered and a recovery made of fundamental truths. God is holy and just and addresses each person with personal choices and possibilities which are not to be ignored and which, when grasped, are aimed at bringing personal hope and fulfilment.

When you live in the land
7. 1–26

This must certainly be regarded as the most difficult and disturbing chapter in the entire book of Deuteronomy, and centres on one of the most fundamental concepts of the religious life – holiness. What does it mean that Israel is a 'holy nation' (cf. Exod. 19. 5)? In seeking to justify and reinterpret this claim Deuteronomy establishes an argument that gives it its most characteristic doctrine – that Israel is a people uniquely chosen by God! A tension arises because Deuteronomy has endeavoured to accommodate the older idea that each nation may have its patron god, or goddess (cf. below on 32. 8–9), with its own conviction concerning the oneness of Israel's God.

The chapter builds upon four major interrelated themes: (i) Israel is a holy people (vv. 1–6); (ii) this holiness is a consequence of God's unique choice (vv. 7–11); (iii) holiness will ensure that Israel enjoys health and prosperity (vv. 12–16); (iv) Israel must not covet the silver and gold of the previous inhabitants of the land, which would undermine and destroy this holiness (vv. 17–26).

The list of the peoples who formed the previous inhabitants of the land (7. 1) is variously given in the Hebrew Bible. Usually they are either six, or seven, in number (cf. Gen. 15. 20; Exod. 3. 8, 17; 13. 5; 23. 23; 33. 2; 34. 11; Deut. 20. 17, etc.). Of the seven names listed some can only partially be identified with known groups and it is evident that a deliberate schematizing has taken place in the lists given. Even those names that are familiar often hide unexplained complexities. The Hittites established a major empire in a region considerably to the north of ancient Palestine (covering a major part of modern Turkey); how a smaller community settled far to the south of this great empire was related to it is unclear. Similarly it remains uncertain why the Canaanites (originally meaning 'traders') gave their name to the land more extensively. The historical picture that emerges from archaeological researches makes it impossible to draw a clear ethnic, or political, map of the settlements in the area at the time of Israel's rise to nationhood. External pressures, particularly from Egypt, and prolonged conflicts between rural and urban communities brought about constant changes of political affiliations and alliances.

35

The call for Israel to exterminate the previous inhabitants (7. 2) has caused the greatest problems for interpreters. Such a demand is out of line with the more reliable historical evidence from elsewhere in the Old Testament that the former population of the land remained a potent influence right up to the time of Judah's collapse in the mid-sixth century BCE.

Moreover much of the language and culture of these peoples was adopted by Israel and played a formative role in the rise of the nation. Clearly the vehemence and intolerance of the Deuteronomic demand that they should be exterminated reflects a depth of anxiety that had positively targeted certain enemies. It may partly reflect a 'crisis of conscience' about past failures, but appears to be directed against surviving groups within the population of whom the Deuteronomists radically disapprove. These were accused of retaining the old customs and religious practices of the pre-Israelite inhabitants and were thereby threatening Israel's 'holiness' as a people. If any explanation at all can be forthcoming to explain the appalling barbarity of the demand it may be sought in the belief that, by undermining Israel's 'holiness', negligence in religious observance brought a major risk of disease. Periods of great social upheaval and military turmoil have, historically, frequently brought plagues which have wiped out whole populations.

From the perspective of the history of biblical interpretation no part of the Old Testament needs to be subjected more carefully to the critical scrutiny of Jesus and the New Testament command to 'Love your enemies; do good to those who hate you' (Matt. 5. 43–48). The New Testament breathes a very different spirit from that which is exemplified in this tragic chapter.

It is surprising in view of this prohibition on intermarriage with the previous inhabitants (v. 3) that the law regarding marriage to a woman taken captive in war is retained in 21. 10–14. In this regard also it is characteristic of the Deuteronomic author to note the influence of the mother on the religious allegiance of children (v. 4), since it consistently recognizes that the household forms a school of education (cf. Prov. 1. 8). The primacy of maternal influence upon high status male children is also evidenced in Prov. 31. 1.

The idea of holiness was drawn from the most basic of Israel's assertions concerning its covenant relationship with the LORD God (Exod. 19. 6). It occupied a primary position among the many terms expressing such a relationship and had a deep-rooted place in the priestly theology regarding the land and its use (cf. 21. 1–9). Yet it is a term to which Deuteronomy accords only a qualified approval, subjecting it to careful revision and affirming a relative place to it. This becomes most evident in the attitude adopted towards Israel's holy places, which are reduced to only one single sanctuary, and the presentation of offerings. The relationship to the LORD God is understood in terms of an inward attitude of obedience, and the purely physical aspects of nearness to God are largely set aside. What Deuteronomy offers is an emphasis upon inward reasoned thinking and self-examination as the essential path to a knowledge of God. Consequently holiness, with its strong associations with ritual and sacred objects and places, is stripped of many of its quasi-physical aspects.

Yet it is not rejected altogether, but is retained, subject to a major reappraisal, being primarily linked to health, prosperity and obedience to the law of God (cf. vv. 12–16). It loses almost all of its physical connotations as a power that may, if wrongly intruded upon, kill the unwary (cf. Num. 16. 1–50; II Sam. 6. 6–8).

The assertion that God had no obvious reason for choosing Israel as a special people (vv. 7–11), except that of a spontaneous love, recognizes the problem of inexplicability that such an assertion expresses. Throughout the book the difficulty in matching the claim that the LORD God of Israel was the only true God with the awareness that other nations worshipped other gods, is strongly evident. Jewish thinking later accommodated the belief that the one and only God could be known by a variety of different names. There is a certain idiomatic restraint present in refusing to be drawn more deeply into attempting to answer an unanswerable question.

The primary focus of attention is found in the Deuteronomic reinterpretation of holiness. Old ideas are retained, but modified by a more closely thought-through reasoning concerning God's life-giving power. Deuteronomy understands holiness most directly of all in regard to health and prosperity (v. 13). So, to a surprising degree for an Old Testament book, the concept is partly secularized. Its traditional quasi-physical aspects largely disappear in the broader affirmation that holiness must be mediated through obedience to God's law and will lead to general health and prosperity.

This was undoubtedly a primary feature of the understanding of holiness from earliest times, but it was intermixed with other concerns of a more directly religious and sacral character. What is remarkable in Deuteronomy is the extent to which it has been given a much narrower focus on questions relating to health, fertility and

37

prosperity more generally. It is this aspect of holiness which is most forcibly presented as an assurance that, by remaining a holy nation, Israel would be protected from all forms of disease. Nowhere else in the Old Testament is this assurance given in quite the categorical fashion that occurs here. Although it contains a relative truth, in the importance that it attaches to aspects of personal hygiene and cleanliness, it evidently lacks a satisfactory understanding of the nature of disease. Sadly, therefore, it represents a feature of Deuteronomy which overstates the situation, and can no longer be upheld. The issue came subsequently to call for closer biblical reflection and is most fully explored in the book of Job, where the belief that disease is a form of divine punishment is categorically rejected. At all levels the mysterious origins of sickness and disease eluded the people of antiquity, even though valuable rules for the promotion of hygiene and health were developed in the biblical laws.

Since Deuteronomy has presented its understanding of God by affirming that there is only one true divine Being the question of the relationship of such a God to non-Israelite nations required to be considered (v. 14). Although the existence of other gods for other nations is not categorically denied, their power is shown as of little worth. Israel's LORD God is Creator of all the earth and rules supreme over all nations.

Consciousness that, in military terms, Israel had shown itself to be unable to fend off the invasions and political intrusions of the great armies of Mesopotamia, is repeatedly evident throughout the book. Undoubtedly the references here to the power to conquer any nation (vv. 17–20) reflect this historical experience. Israel had once been so proud of its military achievements under King David so why had subsequent loss and failure occurred? The assurance given is to look for a deeper level of obedience to the law as a weapon of faith which would override this military failure. Already such an emphasis has been introduced into the stories of the successes gained under the leadership of Moses. This assurance is now carried into a wider sphere with the insistence that a truly wholehearted level of obedience will ensure Israel's victory over any nation.

Not by bread alone
8. 1–10

If the preceding chapter contains many of the most disturbing and unsatisfactory aspects of the teaching of Deuteronomy, so the warmth and depth of spiritual insight of the present one helps to soften this. Here the unfolding story of what Israel had experienced in the years immediately following God's making of the covenant on Mount Horeb is spelt out. These had marked a time of trial and testing which had served to bring out very clearly fundamental truths about the nature of human existence, as it is lived in the light of God's care and presence. These truths are enshrined in a number of memorable phrases which have thereafter become foundations of biblical spirituality. The desolation of the wilderness, through which Israel had struggled throughout a period of forty years, had forced the men and women to experience privation and hunger. Yet they had not starved because God had provided manna for them – enough to live on, and so ensuring survival, but not enough to indulge themselves. Thereby the purpose of the record is . . . *to teach you that people cannot live on bread alone, but that they live on every word that comes from the mouth of the LORD* (v. 3).

So too (vv. 4–10) that generation had had to learn to go without life's luxuries. Old clothes had had to last half a lifetime and the people had had to march shoeless and bootless through the scorching earth. Like children they had been compelled to learn essential truths concerning hardship and discipline which would teach them about 'the real world', with all its many trials. Only so would they then be properly prepared to cope with life and its demands. Accordingly when the nation proceeded into the Promised Land, with all its wealth and richness, these basic truths learned in the harsh circumstances of the wilderness years would forever after provide the people with a heritage of memories never to be forgotten. They were a people who had come *out of that land of slavery* (v. 14). This saga of the nation's origins would then stand it in good stead and the people would know how to enjoy what was good, because they had learned what it was like to go without (v. 10)!

A time to remember
8. 11–20

The Deuteronomists recognized that human memory may be short-lived and the human heart can be deceptively fickle when things are going well (vv. 11–16). It is so easy to forget! So the temptation to complacency and self-approval (v. 14) would always be there, pushing aside the memories of harder times and leading to a sense of well-being that expelled the vital awareness of dependence on the LORD

God. Then the sense of thankfulness that this engendered would be lost.

When this happened it could give rise to the ultimate folly – the belief that one deserved such luxurious living and that it had all been achieved by one's own efforts. The final touch of human pride, leading to disaster, would be to utter the words of a great lie: *My own strength and energy have gained me this wealth* (v. 17). So the conclusion of the address provides us with a most characteristic admonition of Deuteronomy, enshrining all that the book seeks to achieve. It is an incessant urge to *remember the LORD your God* (v. 18), with all that this remembering entails in the way of national history. Knowledge of the past would lead to a right attitude in the present! It gives rise to an admonition tinged with a dire threat if forgetfulness should prevail: *You will be destroyed as surely as were the nations whom the LORD destroyed at your coming* (v. 20). The book was addressed to men and women who were seen to be facing a new national crisis, with the imminent possibility that this terrible threat might become a reality, as Israel once again returned to a new wilderness experience among the nations. What Deuteronomy seeks to spell out is its complete and absolute conviction why such a possibility existed, and why such a disaster might come about: *Because of your disobedience to the LORD your God.*

This rhetorical exploration and personal application of central themes of Israel's historical beginnings make Deuteronomy a preacher's book. It has thereby become the most formative document of the Judaeo-Christian spiritual tradition. It is not history for its own sake, but rather history perceived as disclosing the wisdom of a spiritual way of life. It is history viewed, not from the perspective of national glory and achievement, but from the intensely personal side of human attitude and response. In many ways it is a reversal of the more familiar pattern in which national heroes and leaders are remembered for their great victories, making past glories a substitute for present ills. In Deuteronomic perspective, Moses alone is such a worthy leader and his leadership rests in his resistance to the wavering loyalties and deceptive self-appraisal of the rest of the nation. He forewarns of the dangers which these petty failures will bring. As the nation's troubled beginnings are remembered, so the inner deceptions of human pride and self-approval are repeatedly unmasked.

You are about to cross the Jordan today
9. 1–21

After thirty-eight wasted and painful years had been spent in the wilderness since God had revealed the law on Mount Horeb, at last the time had come for Israel to take decisive action. The warning of Deut. 1. 6 was about to be heeded and a proper response implemented. Israel was now commanded to move ahead and *to occupy the territory of nations greater and more powerful than you* (v. 1). The victories that God brought to the nation when it entered the new land would bring with them an increased temptation to self-congratulation. The very idea of God's special choosing of Israel from among the many nations of the world would carry with it an all-too-real temptation for this divine election to be interpreted as a signal proof of Israel's goodness and virtue. What could go wrong when God was so great and the divine choice so unassailable? The people could feel that they were sure to do well, and even deserved to do so. Yet this would be a travesty of the truth. So the spiritual warning against complacency is reinforced yet again, but, in the process, the very idea of divine election is cast into a new area of mystery and inconsistency. Israel is undeserving and wavering, and the mystery of why God should choose one nation above another is left unanswered. Only as subsequent generations reflected more deeply on the inconsistency of this did the fuller insight of Peter's affirmation in Acts 10. 35–36 stand out. God has no favourites, for to behave in such fashion would contradict the very foundation of divinity – the justice and impartiality of the divine will.

Lest Israel be tempted to challenge the verdict that Israel is, by nature, no more righteous and virtuous than the nations they were about to expel from the land, a further incident from the wilderness years is recalled and its lessons driven home (vv. 8–21). What happened when Israel was left alone during the forty days when Moses had left them leaderless while he ascended Mount Horeb to receive the two tablets of law? Israel had turned with alarming speed to idolatry and thereby had betrayed the very understanding of God which had been so powerfully given to them only days earlier on the mountain! The nation need look no further than the story of its own past to find instructive proof that the human heart is fickle and prone to forget God. Only a few days had been needed for this to happen and even the priestly figure of Aaron had been party to the betrayal

41

(v. 20). Not even priests could wholly be trusted! No, not even the brother of Moses!

The central emphasis of the way the incident is recalled rests on its focus on the speed with which the first and second commandments were broken. The sense of betrayal is shown to be absolute! It is no surprise therefore to reflect that the story of the making of the Golden Calf has become, for artists and storytellers, the archetypical story of human spiritual betrayal. Promises made in a time of excited enthusiasm may be quickly broken the morning after! At the same time the story is important theologically for the focus which it places on the sin of idolatry as the worst form of human affront to God. The choice of a bull-calf image, with all its longstanding associations as a symbol of fertility and sexual power, cannot be overlooked. Undoubtedly too there is a political aspect present in the reproof, since the bull-calf images set up at Bethel and Dan provided a religious focus for the separation of the united Davidic empire into two kingdoms (cf. I Kgs. 12. 25–33). Such images symbolized disloyalty, not only to God, but also to Jerusalem and the royal house of David.

This long-felt, and deeply rooted, antipathy to idolatry expressed in bull-calf images, had already become the central focus of reproach in Israelite tradition before the time of Deuteronomy. Yet Deuteronomy's retelling of the story moves into a deeper level. The idolatry of the making of the Golden Calf, led by no less a figure than Aaron himself, reveals the fickleness, unreliability, and general untrustworthiness of the human heart. The human will is a weak and unreliable instrument for controlling the direction of life – still less of national destiny. There is a warp – a principle of unreliability, that lies buried in the hearts of all human beings. Accordingly a note of deep pessimism concerning human intentions and longing for goodness surfaces here in Deuteronomy. It was later to be more deeply explored by psalmists, by St Paul and by such later theologians as St Augustine and Martin Luther. 'The heart is deceitful.' In this way we discover that Deuteronomy's hostility to idolatry has a deep psychological and personal side to it, which makes it far more than a reflection on contrasting and conflicting views about the value of visual representations of deity.

The treachery of the human heart
9. 22–29

The concluding unit of the chapter expounds this theme of Israel's proneness to disobedience yet more comprehensively: *You were defiant from the day that the Lord first knew you* (v. 24). This is the key text of the chapter, and it is apparent from the emphatic use of the mode of direct address *You were . . .* that its message is not only for the generation who were about to enter the land for the first time, but for every reader of the book. It is intended to disabuse them of any sense of self-pitying despair, and most especially to sweep aside the temptation to blame their own misfortunes upon the misdeeds of past generations. The vain excuse that Israel and Judah were suffering for wrongs carried out by their forbears – most especially Israel's and Judah's fainthearted kings – is swept aside. All have sinned! Only a renewal of loyalty to God's covenant on the part of every surviving Judean who remembered the nation's past could make sure that a different future awaited them. God was faithful. It was the treachery of Israel's proneness to disobey God which was to blame. So the examples of the incidents of past rebelliousness against Moses' leadership had all to be borne in mind. For *Taberah* cf. Num. 11. 1–3 where the name is linked with the idea of burning and associated with God's 'burning' anger against Israel; for *Massah* cf. 6. 16 and Exod. 17. 7; Ps. 95. 8–9; for *Kibroth-hattaavah* cf. Num. 11. 4–34 where the name is linked to Israel's craving for meat in the wilderness. The lessons that these stories brought home were lessons about human rebelliousness and distrust of God. Let every reader take note!

A final touch of rhetorical artistry explores the traditions of the past to bring home the full extent of Israel's faithless behaviour. Since Israel had, from its very beginning, shown itself to be so wavering in its commitment to the LORD God, and unable, even for a few months, to stay away from idolatry, had not the nation's downfall been inevitable from the beginning? The rebuttal of this reasonable contention is forthright. Moses had prayed for the people, setting himself as the mediator between God and nation, and in his prayer, had appealed directly to God to defend his own reputation. Since this was intimately bound up with Israel through the covenant made on Mount Horeb (v. 28), should not God act to uphold the divine honour and reputation? If Israel failed to honour God's covenant, would not the LORD God also have failed? Yet such a line of thought is presented

43

as an unthinkable conclusion to draw. So, ultimately, God's action in protecting Israel, and persevering with the people in spite of all their faults, could be relied upon, since it concerned God's own name and reputation in the world. In many respects the argument is open-ended and inconclusive regarding the implications of the doctrine of God's sovereignty over the nations. Nevertheless, it is this concern to give full weight to the doctrine of the supreme power of the LORD God contrasted with the weakness and fickleness of Israel's faith, that lends to Deuteronomy its note of urgency and openness regarding the future. The future was still to be won, and it is the persistent aim of Deuteronomy to ensure that this future should be won for the side of obedience and trust in the LORD as God.

The law and its custodians
   10. 1–11

After the giving of the Ten Commandments in chapter 5 and the instructions for the central role that it was to play in the future in Israel's life as a daily focus of reflection and commitment (chapter 6), we are now given yet more homilies upon its importance. Attention is focused on the inward and personal temptations that could endanger this priority when the passage of time, and the demands of daily life, encouraged forgetfulness and neglect. Yet certain practical problems remained concerning the law. Where would it be kept so as to guarantee that it was given its rightful place in the nation's worship and rituals, as well as in popular memory? Who would be its custodians so as to ensure that it was available and not changed? The answer to these questions is now set out in 10. 1–9.

The earliest mention of the ark is to be found in Num. 10. 35–36 where it is described as accompanying Israel on their journeyings and is addressed with a battle-cry indicating that God is present with the ark and leads Israel into battle. It was set in the place of greatest honour in the Jerusalem temple after it was built. Its elaborate symbolism has suggested that it was regarded as the throne on which the invisible deity was seated, or even as God's footstool. Deuteronomy presents it as a simple container made of wood which was used to keep the two tablets on which the Ten Commandments were written (v. 3).

On both counts the regulations that are set out have received much attention as reflecting significant shifts in the practical administration of Israel's worship which must be credited to Deuteronomy. They imply subtle changes of interpretation which had become necessary if a new unified charter for all Israel was to be adopted. In some measure these changes can be defended as a concern to restore older practices which had once formed part of the Israelite tradition, chiefly among the northern tribes. These had suffered neglect with that region's political decline since the Assyrian incursions of the eighth century. Deuteronomy was now concerned to integrate these practices into a unified Israelite tradition commensurate with the centring of all worship in Jerusalem. Yet this Jerusalem tradition was also greatly changed and is largely stripped of the triumphalist mythological colouring associated with Mount Zion and the Davidic royal house (cf. Pss. 2, 46, 48).

The most significant explanation for this development is that it shows how the most elaborate features of the royal Zion theology of Jerusalem, with its powerful focus on kingship and the royal house of David, had fallen into disrepute and had lost public credibility. Judah's collapse and Jerusalem's surrender to foreign armies had compelled that Israelite faith in God be given a more reasoned and credible interpretation of Israel's worship and its major institutions. There had to be a more guarded respect for kingship and the temple and their role in Israel's national life.

This becomes extensively evident once we examine closely the rules and interpretations of worship set out in the regulations of chapters 12–15, together with the more cautious attitude towards kingship. Worship itself, with its conventions, taboos and mythological overtones, is subjected to close scrutiny so that actions and rituals that cannot show a reasoned purpose are left aside, or subtly reinterpreted. These changes had been made necessary as a consequence of the events surrounding Judah's political collapse which had brought humiliation to Jerusalem and its temple. The role of the Mosaic law in the life of the nation is now presented as the most central focus of Israel's faith and worship. Those aspects of worship and ritual which do not serve this aim, and promote reflection upon it, are now left aside as no longer important for Israel's relationship to the LORD God. The law of Moses, rather than the temple of Jerusalem, now becomes the central focus of Israel's relationship to God. The covenant declared on Mount Horeb and mediated through Moses forms the central pillar of Israel's existence, so that worship, with its sanctuary priesthood, are there to serve this covenant. Neither temple nor priests will to able to guarantee blessing and God's protection to the people except through obedience to the law.

These principles of worship are here applied to the understanding of the holy ark (10. 3–5), which had once stood in the temple of Jerusalem. When we compare the simple practical function of the ark as described here with the far more elaborate traditions concerning its place as a symbol of the LORD God's presence and leadership in battle (cf. Num. 10. 34–35) we see the wide-ranging nature of Deuteronomy's reinterpretation.

The origin and early status of the Levites has remained a subject of close historical examination and debate, but has resulted in a picture of their earliest social position remaining uncertain. The ruling declared in vv. 8–9 that *Levi has no allotment or inheritance with his kindred* reflects the priestly responsibilities that the Levites carried. For Deuteronomy all Levites appear entitled to full priestly status and priests from no other family are envisaged.

At what time Levi did once form an independent tribe among the others, as biblical tradition asserts, is uncertain, and whether it was ever historically true has been questioned. It may simply be one aspect of the projection back of an original 'ideal' unified family origin for all Israel. Certainly in the historical period Levi's privileged status as priests is emphatically presented, together with an exemplary, if ruthless, loyalty to the Lord as God. Certainly in the earliest period, not all priests were Levites, and it is the Deuteronomic ruling that this should be so that now comes to the fore. The historian of the monarchy notes that this concession was not ultimately established (cf. II Kgs. 23. 9). We find in the period after the disasters of 587 BCE, and especially when worship in a restored temple in Jerusalem recommenced, that not all Levites were permitted to exercise full priestly duties. They formed instead a larger pool of lower-rank temple servants whose duties focused more directly on teaching and instruction in prayer and practical tasks.

The instructions concerning the ark and the Levites serve to confirm the overriding pre-eminence accorded to Israel's covenant law, which has dominated chapters 5–10. This law is now to be the centrepiece of worship. How this is to be conducted will be more fully explained in chapters 12–15. Meanwhile, the singular dependence of Israel on Moses' leadership is reasserted in vv. 10–11, with a further injunction to move ahead to enter the land.

Your own eyes have seen
10. 12–11. 7

The situation envisaged in which Israel is to embark on its great adventure of entering the land promised to its ancestors calls for further reflection on first principles. Only so can it follow the path enshrined in the covenant law. The significant change that the future will bring is that the people will have to live without Moses' presence among them. Instead they will live by the law that Moses brought to them. In this way the leadership which he exercised, and which brought such great victories and triumphs in the beginning, can continue as the guiding principle by which the nation can live and flourish.

In 11. 1–7 the authors display with remarkable rhetorical skill the spiritual direction of the book's purpose. It is focused in the appeal: . . . *you know his great power* (v. 2) . . . *it was you who saw for yourselves* . . . (v. 7). There is a strong sense that every reader is placed in God's moment of choice – today! The generation that perished in the wilderness is left behind as the focus is turned on those who were about to enter the land. But this generation too is merged with the time of the reader, undoubtedly conscious that the nation had not fared well since it entered the land. Yet for each of these generations it is still God's 'today' since the challenge presented by the choice between obedience to the commandments and neglect and forgetfulness of them is still real and present! Each person is heir to the covenant and a privileged custodian of the stories of God's past achievements. Yet this inheritance of knowledge could only be meaningful and effective when rightly acted on in the present. History is important and vital to the nature of the biblical record, but it only becomes God's history when it reaches beyond the past to generate a challenge for the future. God's address to us 'today' is our choice for tomorrow.

Lessons of past failures are not to be forgotten, and the incident recalled in v. 6 concerning the fearsome judgement on Dathan and Abiram, the rebel priests who had rejected the authority of Moses, is told in Num. 16. 1–40. Surprisingly the figure of Korah, who also plays a prominent role in the rebellion, is omitted, almost certainly indicating that the Deuteronomic author possessed the tradition in an earlier version from that now preserved. The details of what happened are recalled only very briefly, but the point is driven home that the carping spirit which called into question Moses' leadership

47

was swiftly dealt with by God. There were lessons from the past, not only of achievement, but also of judgement and disaster.

If you obey . . .
   11. 8–21

The introductory part of Deuteronomy is now brought to a close with a series of reasoned exhortations to keep the commandments which govern Israel's covenant relationship to God. They make a very appropriate conclusion to all that has preceded by bringing to the fore the most prominent of the assumptions that underlie the Deuteronomic understanding of 'life under God's law'. These concern the basic principle that obedience to the commandments and total loyalty to the Lord as God will bring prosperity and success among the nations. Contrastingly disobedience and disloyalty will result in poverty, sickness and national failure. It is a theology based on belief in divine retribution as a practical consequence of living, either for, or against, the way prescribed by God. God helps the faithful and punishes the disobedient.

The opening verses of the chapter list examples of disobedience which God punished severely. Now the prospect of rewards for obedience are set out. Israel's land is portrayed as exceptionally beautiful, fertile and desirable. Its very direct dependence on the regularity of the seasons is emphasized (v. 14) in contrast to Egypt's dependence on the Nile and the need for man-powered irrigation systems (v. 10). Certainly many visitors to the land of Israel, in both ancient and modern times, have been struck by the sharp contrasts between the semi-desert of the south with the lush semi-tropical vegetation of the northernmost parts of it.

Exhortations to make the right choice for God are reiterated in vv. 18–22 in words which recall the central injunctions of chapter 6. The whole of family life is to be coloured by the demand to teach, remember and obey the commandments of God.

Every place where you set foot will be yours
   11. 22–32

The rewards for obedience are reaffirmed in strikingly optimistic terms concerning Israel's future greatness and the limits to which its future boundaries will extend are described in quite remarkable breadth (vv. 24–25). How far this represents an 'ideal' coverage, based on the aspirations nurtured by King David's successes, and how far it is a rhetorical exaggeration outlining what was thought possible, is not clear. The two mountains situated opposite the sanctuary of Gilgal, where a major crossing-point of the River Jordan was located, are then presented as typifying the choices facing Israel – blessing, or curse. It is for you to choose, is the verdict which the author boldly affirms!

The entire section is instructive for the fundamental issues regarding religion, morality and human well-being which are raised. Law-abiding, God-loving conduct, which conforms closely, and where necessary ruthlessly, to the demands of God's covenant is promised rich rewards of health, happiness and prosperity. Conversely, departure from these standards is threatened with dire punishments, with no escape. It is a starkly presented contrast which has undoubtedly served to shape and colour much popular religious life, based as it is on the biblical foundation set out here. But is it true? Can religious loyalty and faith be sure of such rewards in this life as are set out here?

Undoubtedly a great majority of persons who have reflected on the experiential, scientific and theological basis for adhering to such promises and warnings in the modern world, reject them. At best it leads to a self-interested and self-serving type of religion, and at worst it leads to dangerous illusions when ill-health, disappointment and difficulties are encountered. 'Why me?' becomes the cry of the unfortunate sufferer. In any case, the extent of social interrelatedness in wider economic, political and natural disasters, such as earthquakes and drought, means that individual persons, and even communities, are not judged in such a simplistic and personal fashion. Modern environmental problems and sensitivities have shown the extent to which many major threats are the shared responsibility of whole communities and nations.

In defence of the Deuteronomic belief in this certainty of divine retribution, which colours so strongly the book of Deuteronomy, certain aspects of it need to be reflected on. Perhaps at the head of such reflection it is important to note that so much that follows Deuteronomy in both the Old and New Testaments, represents a fuller, and more profound, exploration of the issues raised. The torments of such prophets as Jeremiah, as well as the story of Job and the whole tradition of religious martyrdom, engage more deeply with the conflict between just rewards and the realities of life which are focused in this section. As a platform on which deeper reflection can build the expectation is important to note. As a truth about the reality of human existence it is woefully limited.

There are, nevertheless, important concerns which are touched upon in the Deuteronomic assurances regarding blessing and curse which demand closer scrutiny. First among these we need to set the awareness of a relationship between human beings and their natural environment, which is described with such proverb-like confidence here. The natural world is itself a very complex reality, which cannot be disturbed and exploited with impunity. Belief in its divine design and providential oversight, warn us firmly against such human arrogance. Past mistakes have increased modern awareness of the extent to which the earth's resources are limited. Rain-forests, mineral wealth and fossil fuels are not limitless. They cannot be exploited for the benefit of a few, and without limit, since they are a divine trust. The responsibilities of humankind do not imply that God has simply handed over the world for humankind to use, or abuse, at will.

A second issue that is raised by the Deuteronomic assurances regarding blessing and curse relates to the very direct way in which health and holiness are presented as interconnected. Modern understanding of the complex origin of disease counsels us not to make the mistake of supposing that commitment to faith and religious loyalty will ensure freedom from illness and physical handicap. It is a feature of Deuteronomy which needs to be seen in a historical perspective that it binds together truths about the natural world, and the origin of disease, which can no longer be upheld precisely as they are set out. Nor can the assumption be made that faith and prayer will always provide a path to health and healing.

Nevertheless, it is also necessary to keep in mind that religious faith and health are not wholly separate. A spiritual life-style, of the kind that is so emphatically commanded in Deuteronomy, recognizes the wholeness of human life and the closeness of the relationship between physical and spiritual health. It counsels the need for a submissive and trusting attitude in matters that cannot otherwise be personally controlled. It affirms the necessity of cultivating an attitude of love and responsibility, both towards God and human neighbours, if life is to be lived to the full.

In a third aspect the teaching of Deuteronomy marks a significant, and path-finding, new dimension in human understanding. The description of the two mountains, Gerizim and Ebal, as symbolizing respectively blessing and curse, and the linking of both to human responsibility for choosing between obedience and disobedience

50

to the moral law of God, dispels a whole world of taboo-ridden fears regarding misfortune and ill-health. The ancient world was permeated deeply with beliefs that power-charged words, lucky charms and amulets, and a complex multiplicity of mystical prayers were the key to securing prosperity and happiness or misfortune and disaster. Blessings and curses were thought to possess an inner power of their own; those who were capable of uttering them, thereby gained a fear-based authority. Much of ancient society was a paradise for fortune-tellers, since life was often precarious.

Deuteronomy repudiates all such taboo-ridden thinking concerning religion by subjecting all life and all its eventualities to the law of God. Not demons and magic, but the covenant-law given through Moses, was the key to the quality of life. Understanding the real world, and shouldering the moral responsibilities that the human condition inevitably brings, offers a reasoned and reasonable path for living. Thereby knowledge of the Mosaic law removes any need to foster, or ward off, the forces of a hostile supernatural world. At one stroke this Deuteronomic doctrine, exaggerated as it undoubtedly is concerning the directness of divine rewards and retribution, dispels many of the conventional taboos and fears of popular religion.

Part II

The Deuteronomic Law Code

12.1–26.19

We now begin a new, and formally very different, section of the book which calls for a separate introduction. It consists of a series of regulations, instructions and laws of the kind that prescribe a pattern of social life and religious observance as well as determining in many cases the kind of action called for in a court of law. With the rise of modern critical scholarship, this law book has frequently been regarded as the earliest, and most original, part of Deuteronomy. This has, in turn, led to the belief that, if indeed some part of Deuteronomy was the 'law book of Moses' that initiated the major civil and religious reforms of King Josiah (II Kgs. 22–23), then it was probably this section. However, before attempting any judgement on such an issue some important aspects of the content of what is set out in chapters 12–26 need to be considered.

The first concerns the close relationship which is evident between this Deuteronomic law book and an earlier list of laws of a similar nature in Exod. 20. 22–23. 19 which is usually called 'The Book of the Covenant'. Close comparison of the two shows that the Deuteronomic code represents a revision and expansion of the Exodus law book which must therefore have been earlier in its time of origin. Much interest attaches to the changes introduced since they reflect a concern for greater fairness in the application of the law, achieving greater effectiveness in its use and expanding its range. They show the direction of the refining and development of legal thinking and procedures which has continued on into the rise of modern legal systems. Discerning the reasons for the biblical changes therefore proves very instructive.

A second aspect of the Deuteronomic laws of chapters 12–26 has more recently come to the forefront and concerns the extent to which the order of the legislation follows closely the order of the Ten Commandments. The connections can be set out in the following manner:

52

The First Commandment.	Deut. 12. 1–13. 18. Worship of other gods besides the LORD God of Israel is not to be tolerated.
The Second Commandment.	Deut. 14. 1–21. God's name is to be honoured.
The Third Commandment.	Deut. 14. 22–16. 17. The sabbath is to be observed.
The Fourth Commandment.	Deut. 16. 18–18. 22. Respect for parents and civil authority is to be maintained.
The Fifth Commandment.	Deut. 19. 1– 22. 8. Rules for the protection of life.
The Sixth Commandment.	Deut. 22. 9–23. 18. Rules governing natural boundaries.
The Seventh Commandment.	Deut. 23. 19–24. 7. Protection of property.
The Eighth Commandment.	Deut. 24. 8–25. 4. Prohibition of perjury.
The Ninth Commandment.	Deut. 25. 5–12. Protection of the family.
The Tenth Commandment.	Deut. 25. 13–26. 15. Prohibition of all selfish and excessive desire.

At first glance the directness of the link with the Ten Commandments does not always appear obvious, but it becomes more readily apparent once it is recognized that certain issues, such as that of maintaining respect for parents, serve as a heading to introduce a wider range of related issues concerning public and civil authority. Similarly some attempt to introduce linking elements between the various groups is apparent, as can be seen in 22. 9–12 relating to hidden boundaries of the natural world. This ordering of the laws to follow the pattern of the commandments appears as a relatively late effort at establishing an overall shape to the law code. In principle, however, it is of considerable significance since it highlights the fact that the commandments did not stand apart from, or instead of, a more formal legal system, but the two were designed to work together. In many respects the specific laws defining religious observance, family structures, civil offences and crimes gave definition and direction to the commandments which inevitably extended to cover a very broad range of concerns. Right action in protecting persons against criminal activity and abuse required to be based on a right attitude towards God and the community more generally. Much the same point is made in Lev. 19. 18 where the famous dictum *you must love your neighbour as yourself* occurs in the midst of a list of commandments. Good laws need a right attitude to apply and uphold them!

A third issue is also relevant in regard to the law code of Deuteronomy 12–26. This concerns the extent to which it reveals a familiarity with comparable laws from Assyria and the ancient Near East generally. There can be no question that lists of laws, of the kind which provided a basis for a state-administered, largely secular, legal system emerged in ancient Mesopotamia. Such laws have proved to be one of the world's greatest civilizing achievements. Both Israel's Book of the Covenant and the Deuteronomic law book show a degree of familiarity with such ancient Mesopotamian laws. There is much evidence to suggest therefore that Josiah's major legal revival and reorganization in Jerusalem (cf. II Kgs. 22. 3–23. 25) drew upon knowledge of the ancient Assyrian tradition. It was one of the gains which accrued from Judah's centuries of subservience to Mesopotamia.

At all three levels therefore, of comparison with the earlier Israelite Book of the Covenant of Exod. 20. 22–23. 19, with the Ten Commandments of Deut. 5. 6–21 and with the now recovered ancient Near-Eastern lists of laws, there is much material with which to compare the Deuteronomic code of laws.

Study of the wide range of relationships between these collections of ancient laws helps to set in perspective several of the questions which have often been addressed to Deuteronomy. Foremost here is the question of the date of Deuteronomy's law code and the issue whether it forms the oldest part of the present book. Certainly this is unlikely to be the case, since, like any effective working law book, close study of Deuteronomy shows that revisions and expansions were made to the wording of laws and to arrangements for administering them in order to meet changing circumstances. Most especially the collapse of Judah's central government (and legal) administration after the Babylonian destruction of Jerusalem in 587 BCE necessitated great changes and reorganization. So there is much in the present book which is best understood as introduced in the wake of this catastrophe, while other parts must antedate it. Never before had the general welfare and survival of Israel's faith and moral health been as severely tested as occurred during the sixth century BCE. It is not surprising therefore that a sense of social and moral crisis is reflected in the book, with more than one way of dealing with certain basic problems being sought.

This awareness helps also to answer the question, long considered in detail by biblical scholars, about the relationship of the Deuteronomic law book to that reported as recovered during Josiah's administrative reform in 621 BCE. Was any part of Deuteronomy that book? What becomes clear is that Josiah's action marked the beginning of an important sequence of developments which were introduced in Jerusalem, but which afterwards needed to be revised and adapted in the wake of the political turmoil which the following century brought. At what point in this century of change particular features of the Deuteronomic law are to be dated is usually impossible to answer, and in the long run is of little importance.

What comes through is the genuine sense of realism which pervades Deuteronomy as a book of 'living' law and legislative activity. The need to fall back on basic principles, to maintain freedom and compassion whilst holding off threatened anarchy and moral chaos is constantly apparent. The temptation to issue laws dealing with almost everything when there was no realistic possibility of maintaining them had to be resisted. So there had often to be an appeal to adopt a right attitude of compassion and fairness towards the underprivileged groups such as resident foreigners and slaves. Their chance of having recourse to the law courts was virtually non-existent. At the same time, when the very foundations of all moral order appeared on the point of collapse, there was always the temptation to threaten fierce and draconian punishments, calling on fear in order to maintain a semblance of civilized order. So Deuteronomy's laws often show surprising, and seemingly conflicting, contrasts between compassion and ruthlessness. When seen in context the book forces us to think deeply about responsibility for the roles of religion and freedom in society.

Rules of Worship
12. 1–16. 17

The law of the central sanctuary
12. 1–4

Coming first in the law code, as it does, the law regarding the setting up and operation of a single place of worship to which the offerings and sacrifices for the LORD God are to be brought, marks one of the brand marks of Deuteronomic policy-making. It lays down the practical ways in which the obligations of the First Commandment are to be expressed. The section falls quite smoothly and conveniently into four parts, in which an original central demand has been built on and added to. Yet these separate requirements fit closely together and all have as their goal the fulfilling of the commandment that the LORD God alone is to be worshipped.

Older, non-Israelite, places of worship, with all their religious symbols and bric-a-brac, were to be completely destroyed (vv. 1–4). Thereby the temptation to worship other gods, or to worship the LORD as God with alien and misleading symbols, would be removed. Clearly Deuteronomy was determined to enforce a much stronger attitude over this issue which had, from the evidence of the rebukes of the prophets against popular idolatry and Baal worship, never been very resolutely applied. So long as people had worshipped at the major sanctuaries for the major festivals priestly tolerance of a continuing worship at age-old rural sanctuaries and altars had been commonplace. That tolerance was no longer to be maintained.

The right place for worship
12. 5–12

Henceforth Israel was to worship only at the one place designated as *the place which the LORD your God will choose out of all your tribes to receive his name that it may dwell there*. The distinctive wording evidently marks a reformulation of the older law of the altar in Exod. 20. 24 and is striking on account of the way in which God's 'name' appears as a manifestation of God's very presence. It marks a feature of Deuteronomy that God is described as 'present' at the sanctuary not in a physical manner, which the older tradition described as the 'presence' (the Hebrew is literally 'face') of the deity, but as open to be called upon through prayer and to receive praise. So God's availability at the sanctuary is affirmed without supposing that there was anything physical about the divine presence there, but only the divine 'name'.

Clearly from the time when the Jerusalem temple was built this designated sanctuary was Jerusalem, but it was important for Deuteronomy to affirm the tradition that such a divine presence had accompanied Israel from the time of Moses through the ark and the tabernacle. The destruction of the Jerusalem temple by the Babylonians in 587 BCE quite evidently dealt a terrible blow to the reputation and credibility of that tradition. Nevertheless it was vital for Deuteronomy to insist that, even though the temple had been

56

destroyed, Jerusalem alone was the sole approved location to which offerings and sacrifices could be brought. There could be no temple built, nor altar erected, in some other place than Jerusalem. This ruling was later to have far-reaching consequences for the whole character and development of Jewish worship which eventually led to the setting aside of special lay places of assembly (synagogues) for prayer and instruction.

The right way to worship
12. 13–19

As a result of this restriction there were major consequences concerning the way in which animals were slaughtered for a festival meal. Hitherto virtually all such killing had been a sacral act, since it involved the shedding of blood. In future modified arrangements would be necessary to allow for animal slaughter outside of this religious setting. Accordingly the slaughter of animals for food was to be permitted as a secular, non-religious, activity, in the same manner that deer and similar animals were slaughtered in the hunt (vv. 13–19). This was not to dispense with the special offerings to God of the tithes and firstlings of domestic animals, which were still to be brought to the approved sanctuary and used for a shared community meal (vv. 17–19).

The profane slaughter of animals
12. 20–28

The restrictions relating to sacrificial meals also had consequences for the secular slaughter of domestic animals simply for food without any special religious meaning. Such action was now to be separated from the more specific religious purpose of making gifts to the deity. However even these also took on a wider purpose and should be used to show support for the Levites – the priestly servants of the sanctuary – and used as a means of reinforcing household solidarity. This could be achieved by inviting the entire household, including slaves, to join in the meal as an opportunity of rejoicing together (vv. 18–19). So ordinary domestic meals would fulfil a sacred purpose through the expression of compassion, solidarity and family rejoicing. Every meal could be a holy event!

The ruling here is significant since it marks a major step towards the secularizing of the act of slaughtering a domestic animal, provided that the blood was disposed of separately and not consumed. Previously all forms of taking of life, even of relatively small creatures, had been carefully subjected to religious restraints since the life of every animal was seen ultimately as a gift of God (cf. the special ruling affirmed in Gen. 9. 1–6 after Noah had saved the animal realm from the ravages of the Great Flood). The fact that special concessions had been necessary for hunting wild animals is here made into a precedent for a wider change of practice.

It was essential that lay persons should be absolutely clear regarding the distinction between sacrificial offerings and domestic slaughter (vv. 20–28). At the back of this distinction, which has had widespread consequences for Jewish and Christian worship and dietary practice, lies an awareness that the restriction of all offerings to one specified altar would certainly create difficulties for some loyal citizens. In many instances the distance required to travel would be too great, especially when animals and cereal offerings had to be carried. So the ruling of Deuteronomy frees the slaughtering of animals for food from the religious restraints which otherwise pertained to the offering of animals for sacrifice at the sanctuary.

Thereby two kinds of animal slaughter became commonplace, whereas previously profane killing in the hunt had alone been exempt from the sacral rules. It was necessary therefore that lay persons should be familiar with the rules which applied to each of them. Both were necessary, and the introduction of the less restrictive procedure when no priestly presence was required, was not to lead to the discontinuance of the longstanding tradition of making appropriate offerings at the central sanctuary in their proper season. Both formal religious observance and less formal domestic meals were each to have their place. In time it is remarkable that Judaism has developed a careful body of informal rules regarding family meals which has made even secular meals into an expression of religious loyalty. Much Jewish home-life has therefore developed in a manner which has been termed 'domestic spirituality'.

From a historical perspective these rules regarding the central sanctuary point us to the origins of the law book of Deuteronomy in a period of crisis when Israel's Mosaic inheritance of faith and religious observance was put to a severe test as a result of the imperial conquests of Assyria and Babylonia. The ultimate disaster had been the destruction of the Jerusalem temple in 587 BCE and the disruption of priestly administration which followed this. Dire events called for far-reaching remedies, and the need to uphold the authority of

Jerusalem and its tradition was paramount, even though the city lay in ruins. Nevertheless, behind the rules which were drawn up and are preserved here, we discern some of the most long-lasting and vital issues for all faith to consider. We may briefly note what these issues are.

Heading the list we should certainly note the importance which is attached to maintaining a harmony and positive interaction between formal public worship and private devotion in the home focused on the family and its traditions. Public worship ought to provide a model for private prayers and personal devotion. The preserved biblical psalms are the evident testimony to this since they are formal and expertly composed, yet intended to provide a basis for private devotion. At the same time it is clear that much of Israel's early family household religion (cf. Jer. 7. 17–18) was often crude, taboo-ridden, and filled out with myths and imagery which often had a dangerous sexual emphasis. The loss of the temple could only serve to revive and encourage a return to such private religious activities. So Deuteronomy strove hard, and sometimes ruthlessly (cf. chapter 13), to deal with this situation by maintaining a strong emphasis upon the importance of the central sanctuary as the controlling authority for worship and all that accompanied it. At the same time it recognized the need and value of a strong tradition of household piety. It encouraged this by urging reflection at home on God's law (cf. Deut. 6. 7) while allowing the slaughter of animals for food to become a purely secular, non-religious activity. Public and private piety were to go hand in hand.

A second aspect of this Deuteronomic ruling about worship concerns the implications of its formal introduction of a division between the sacred and the secular. If we could rethink our way into the earliest mental outlook of Israel it would certainly be to rediscover the awareness that religious ideas and imagery permeated every aspect of life and human activity. Birth and death, the practice of agriculture, even the notions and definitions of space and time, were all understood in regard to the 'holiness' of human existence. The claim that Israel was itself a 'holy nation' (cf. Exod. 19. 5–6) formed a part of this world-view. In biblical perspective it is undoubtedly the book of Deuteronomy which first moves strongly in the direction of making a sharper distinction between the sacred and the secular. With the spread of exiled Jews among many nations in what has come to be termed 'the Dispersion' this distinction became more important than ever, making it easier for Jews to come to terms with living among communities practising diverse religions. So there were ultimately gains and losses in the changes that Deuteronomy brought. In general, however, it may be claimed that such changes had become inevitable in the face of actual events in Judah.

Since the end of the eighteenth century no feature has characterized the place of religion in Western society more than this increasing separation between the secular and the sacred. It has been in step with the rise of modern science and a scientific world-view and has led to a fresh regard for religious commitment as a matter of personal choice and allegiance. Faith and devotion have themselves come increasingly to be regarded as matters of a private and personal nature, leaving wider views of society and the world to a more neutral, secular perspective. So the spiritual life has itself come increasingly to be expressed privately and to be focused on inward and personal reflection.

It is formal public worship that has struggled to maintain itself. In this regard we can appreciate the two-sided dimension of Deuteronomy. At its heart lies a deep concern to establish a tightly regulated 'official religion'. Yet, in doing so, it also introduces a new emphasis on individual reflection and instruction in the home, on remembering the past as a way of maintaining faith and on the nurture of right attitudes towards fellow citizens. Its aim overall is to reinforce the bond between 'official' religion (Jerusalem with its temple and priesthood) and private worship. Much of the background to this is to be found in the setbacks which had overtaken Israel's major traditional religious institutions. The danger was that these setbacks would lead to a revival of interest in the older family gods and household rituals, which Deuteronomy so deeply distrusted. In their place there was a need for a new 'sanctifying' of ordinary domestic life based on teaching and prayer focused on why worshipping the LORD as God meant pursuing justice and compassion.

Punishment for acts of religious disloyalty
12. 29–13. 18

Once again, as we found between chapters 7 and 8, a set of instructions which appear to have a very positive and praiseworthy intention is followed by a further set of laws of a very different character. These are, nevertheless, closely connected in purpose with those that have preceded them. They are set out in four main sections:

1) 12. 29–32   The covenant introduces the threat of punishment and curse as well as blessing. The theme is dealt with extensively throughout 12. 1–28. 68.
2) 13. 1–5   The threat from prophets and interpreters of dreams who are guilty of incitement to worship other gods is to be countered by imposing the death penalty.
3) 13. 6–11   Incitement to act similarly from members of one's family or close friends, is not to be exempted from punishment in this fashion.
4) 13. 12–18   Any town which displays such disaffection and apostasy is to be totally destroyed by burning. All its inhabitants are to be killed and everything in it, including the livestock, is to be destroyed. Such wholesale destruction in the interests of maintaining the first commandment to worship the LORD God alone is interpreted as constituting a whole burnt offering (v. 16). This town is then to be left a ruin and never rebuilt!

The draconian severity of the measures demanded is breathtaking in its awfulness. Nor can we feel comfortable with the way in which such ruthless steps are to be implemented, since the raising of such accusations actually encouraged that a citizen should inform against a spouse or other family member. The risks that this might be done with false and malicious intent called for a further treatment of the subject in Deut. 17. 6–7; 22. 25–27. This draws attention to the need to ensure that any such charges were safeguarded with the same cautions regarding truthful evidence which applied to cases of murder and rape. Verse 11 makes it clear that these severe penalties for proven cases of religious disaffection were intended to have an intimidatory effect upon the entire community.

In recoiling with alarm at these laws for upholding the first commandment, some reflection upon their historical context is in order. In the first instance, it is evident that the uncompromising severity of the punishments imposed, and the treatment of religious apostasy as a kind of infection which required to be 'purged' from the community like a disease (v. 5), reflects a very distinctive way of looking at such offences. They are not seen as 'crimes' in the familiar sense, but as an affront to God and thereby incurring a threat to the religious foundation of the community. We cannot altogether rule out the suspicion that a fear of disease, brought by those who did not observe the rules of 'holiness' (= hygiene) has helped to motivate such an attitude. Those who broke the strict restraints on the protection of the

61

nation's 'holiness' were believed to be putting at risk the health of the community as a whole.

From a historical perspective it is not at all clear how far these laws were carried into effect by Jewish authorities in Old Testament times. The religious allegiance of Jews living in Judah after the Jerusalem temple had been destroyed was evidently very mixed and the situation for the growing numbers living outside the land in the situation in dispersed communities was even more uncertain. Prophetic rebukes and threats from this period point to the widespread popular return to forms of undesirable private cults and activities which cannot have been readily curbed. Moreover much of the success of the emerging Judaism of the exile rested in its flexibility and a reasonable level of tolerance in the face of the many social and religious difficulties experienced. So it is likely that the severe punishments threatened here were seldom carried out and that the Jewish administration, acting under Persian, and later Greek, oversight, was seldom in a position to act violently in order to preserve observance of the first commandment.

Nevertheless, such historical reflection does little to lessen the modern repugnance felt towards such a desire to enforce religious obedience by resorting to cruel punishments and death. Far too tragic a history exists, especially in Western Christian countries, of attempts to enforce laws demanding religious allegiance by Christian governments. Such measures gave rise to the European burning of supposed 'witches', the Spanish Inquisition and to a long line of martyrs, Jewish, Christian and Muslim. Not until the late seventeenth century CE, after two centuries of intermittent conflict and persecution in Europe, was a strongly reasoned case for religious tolerance established as a feature of the British way of life. No factor has more strongly encouraged the growth of the secular state than the past oppressive behaviour of avowedly Christian governments. That these Deuteronomic laws have frequently been cited in support of attempts to enforce religious conformity highlights their dangerous nature. At best their presence in the Bible may be recognized as a reason for reflecting on the issue of the nature of religious freedom and the right and duty of governments to promote, and where necessary restrict, religious observance. How far should the tolerance of a modern secular state be stretched? Clearly some forms of religious activity may be regarded as socially harmful. At other times they may become politically subversive.

62

The holiness of God's name: life and death
   14. 1–21

The section that now follows in the Deuteronomic law book begins
(v. 1) and ends (v. 21) with regulations which concern the need to
maintain a closely observed distinction between life and death. The
underlying key concept is expressed in v. 2 *you are a people holy to the
LORD your God* which provides us with the clue to understanding what
lies behind the rulings set out. They are designed to protect and
promote the holiness of Israel as God's people, which is itself a way of
upholding the holiness of God's name.

The description of Israel as *children of the LORD your God* (v. 1) retains
an ancient concept which is now clearly regarded as a metaphor for
Israel's covenant relationship to God. This relationship requires that
Israel refrain from trafficking with death, or the dead. The minor
forms of self-mutilation in the presence of a dead person listed are
regarded as misguided concessions to the power of death (regarded
as a distinct deity called Mot in Canaanite religion). They are usually
interpreted as a typified 'disguise' to dissuade death from taking yet
another victim.

In comparable fashion the seemingly pointless and bizarre ritual of
boiling the kid of a goat in its mother's milk (v. 21) prohibits a ritual
which mixed life with death in an unwarrantable way and which was
apparently popularly thought to have special power to promote
fertility and ward off the threat of disease (cf. also Exod. 23. 19). The
prohibition which precedes this is more readily intelligible since it
precludes the eating of any animal carcase which had died of its
own accord and had not been properly slaughtered (cf. the earlier
formulation in Exod. 22. 31). The willingness to allow it to be given
to an 'alien' (the Hebrew *ger* refers to a person of foreign origin
permanently living in the community), or to be sold to a complete
foreigner (the Hebrew for this is *nokri*) is a striking reflection of the
social stratification felt in ancient Israelite society based on ancient
ethnic loyalties.

Overall we can see clearly that the setting out of these regulations is
based on a concern to maintain Israel's holiness by ruling out con-
tamination through the presence of death. This is exemplified not
only in the carcases of dead animals, where the cause of death was
unknown, but by the practice of customs and actions which treated
death as a hostile supernatural power. Such restraint becomes

explicable in view of the portrayal of Mot as a deity of death in Canaanite mythology (we may compare Isaiah's ironic rebuke of those who 'made a covenant with death' in Isa. 28. 15). In between (vv. 4–20) we have a list of clean and unclean creatures which corresponds closely to the comparable list in Lev. 11. 1–45.

The unclean creatures mentioned in v. 3 are said to constitute *an abominable thing* which offends God. The term is elsewhere used of conduct, as well as objects, which are repugnant to God. Scholars regard the list as having been compiled, almost certainly in successive stages, from a list of ten clean animals (vv. 4–5) which has been followed by a list of ten unclean birds, and then amplified by a list of a further ten unclean birds taken from Lev. 11. 13–19.

On first reading such a chapter appears to have more for the ornithologist than the preacher, but closer examination well repays the effort. When seen in a biblical context, and set against modern Christian usage, few words have given rise to greater changes, or caused greater difficulties, than has that of holiness.

The idea of holiness is certainly one of the most fundamental features of religious experience, both ancient and modern. Recognition of this fact was the subject of a major twentieth-century work of theology by Rudolf Otto entitled *The Idea of the Holy* in which human response to holiness as a sense of 'mystery, otherness' was regarded as the basic groundwork of religion. In line with this anthropologists have shown great interest in the present chapter, illustrating as it does the many-sided aspects of holiness in its biblical setting. A primary feature lies in the relatively marginal link between holiness and good conduct. From a basic sense of separation and mysteriousness the idea of holiness progressed only gradually and incompletely to describe good, law-abiding, conduct. Primarily it denotes an association with divine power and a consequent separation from ordinary everyday profane activities and things. Only when emphasis was placed on God as being supremely good, did holiness come to signify a 'godly', in the sense of morally good, way of living. Even today the adjective 'holy' conveys a confused and uncertain meaning to many people.

In examining Deut. 14 we see immediately that Israel's holiness was closely linked to a sharp contrast between life and death. Already chapter 7 has introduced a detailed presentation of the Deuteronomic understanding of what it means for Israel to be 'a holy nation'. A prominent feature of that interpretation is its close linking of holiness with health and of uncleanness with disease. Holiness was what promoted and protected life, since death was itself an experience shrouded in mystery and naturally arousing fear when it struck, sometimes unexpectedly. Moreover death was not simply the passing of a final frontier into another world, but a force which was regarded as actively and presently threatening in this world through disease, famine and other forces of destruction. Seen against such a background we can understand why the present chapter brings together rules concerning forbidden funerary rituals (v. 1), discrimination between safe and unsafe meat, the avoidance of rotting animal carcases (v. 21), as well as a rejection of strange potions aimed at promoting fertility (v. 21). All of them have in common the potential presence of death. Against this the holiness implicit in living as God's people is concerned with the protection and preservation of life in all its many forms.

If the chapter still retains an important lesson for us to ponder it lies in its recognition of the wholeness of life and the belief that such wholeness is itself a God-given gift and that faith integrates our many concerns with health, mental well-being, happiness, safe food and freedom from the disabling fear of death. Seeking holiness should not be a flight from the real world of daily living, but learning to deal with it, to cope with its uncertainties and risks, and finding in holiness a pathway to a fuller enjoyment of life in all its God-planned potential.

The holiness of God's name: time
14. 22–15. 23

A seeming miscellany of rulings and directions appear together in this section and it is only when we look beneath the surface to seek a common connecting thread that we find one. In this case it lies in upholding a recognition of the holiness of God's name in regard to the passage of time. The section, which contains five units, can be understood as extended from the primary command to *observe the sabbath day and keep it holy* (Deut. 5. 12). As observance of the sabbath as a day of rest and worship marked the most basic way of acknowledging the holiness of time, so other time divisions called for appropriate responses in order to uphold awareness that they also involved human relationships with God. These time divisions were experienced first of all in respect of the seasons of the agricultural year and it comes as no surprise therefore to find that the first unit deals with the produce of the fields (14. 22–29) and the last with the increase of flocks and herds (15. 19–23).

Awareness of the seasons of agriculture brought into consideration questions about debts (15. 1–6), the need for compassion towards a poor neighbour (15. 7–11) and the consequent issue of slavery (15. 12–17), since by far the majority of slaves fell into such misfortune as a result of debts, either their own or that of their family. There is therefore a greater level of connection between the separate rulings than might at first appear and underlying the first four of them there is a major concern with poverty and the need for assistance towards those who had not benefited from the increase of fields and herds as had their more fortunate fellow-citizens. The passage of time bore out the truth of the old adage 'time means money', but, whereas most were expected to have prospered, others would not have done so for various reasons. Their plight was to be alleviated and it was in actions for relieving the impact of poverty that the passing of time would be rendered 'holy'. As a holy nation Israel was to be a family community (the 'member of your community' of 15. 7 is literally described as 'a brother', indicating this family ideal for Israel's life as a nation; the REB less happily translates as 'one of your fellow-countrymen').

Looked at in detail the five subjects covered by this list of rulings appear as follows:

Tithes
14. 22–29

The origin of the practice of setting aside a one-tenth portion of the produce of the fields – grain, wine and oil – reaches far back behind Old Testament times into the very beginnings of the cultivation and planting of the soil. Since the land was itself regarded as ultimately divinely owned (cf. Lev. 25. 23), and its cultivation dependent upon the divine gifts of rain and sun, it was necessary that a carefully defined part of all its produce should be returned to the divine Owner. Thus it was at one time looked upon very much as a form of divine 'tax' returned for the use of the deity. This in turn was usually understood to allow its use by the sanctuary personnel (Levites). Wider charitable sharing with the poor of the community was also allowed. Accordingly a special 'third-year' tithe is called for here in which this charitable purpose of the tithe is further emphasized (vv. 28–29).

The most striking and innovative feature of this Deuteronomic ruling lies in vv. 24–26 which makes a distinctive concession in order to take account of geographical limitations imposed by having only

66

one central sanctuary. Clearly for many citizens to carry their tithes there would prove impracticable so allowance is made for the conversion of the actual tithe into money, which could then later be spent on suitable food at the central sanctuary during an act of worship. The very reference to the use of money (usually silver) as a means of exchange reveals the emergence of a new stage of social and economic development in Israel. The significant feature is that it is no longer the tithe itself, regarded as physically holy, but rather the value of the tithe as the means for a celebratory meal to which were invited the entire household, together with the Levites of the sanctuary. What mattered was the inner spiritual value of acknowledging God's gift of the crops, sharing them in a joyful act of celebration, and extending this to those who were God's servants.

Once again a distinctive feature of Deuteronomic 'theologizing' comes to the fore in which the traditional respect for holiness is retained, but subjected to modifications and adaptation to enable it to be applied in a situation which might have compelled it to lapse. It marks yet another step in the distinctiveness of Deuteronomy which led on the one hand to a more rational and inward-looking attitude to religious observance. On the other hand this 'modernizing' tendency also served as a step in the direction of affirming a less physical and ritualistic understanding of what constituted a holy activity. Thereby spiritual meaning was carried across into very simple humanitarian activities focused on a celebratory meal. In the longer term such moralizing and humanizing of ritual aspects of holiness came to be developed into a vital spiritual principle which has remained fundamental to Jewish and Christian tradition (cf. Mark 7. 14–15). It is not 'things in themselves' which are either holy or profane, but the way in which such objects are used to express a relationship to God.

The remission of debts
15. 1–6

The ruling set out here has proved very puzzling to commentators who have wondered how it could ever have worked in practice. Every seventh year all debts incurred during the previous six years were to be allowed to lapse. The term 'remission' specifically means 'letting go' and the term has undoubtedly been carried over from agricultural practice in which a rotation of fields was practised. Every seventh year one field would be 'let go' and left fallow.

67

Compassion for the poor
15. 7–11

The admonitory note in these verses has evidently been included because rules concerning loans and their repayment raised questions about the need for such help. It is throughout assumed that they would be to assist an impoverished neighbour who had encountered hard times, and were not intended as supporting commercial ventures. So the injunction against 'mean thinking' which is outlined in verses 7–9 is aimed at encouraging a willingness to help those in trouble. It incidentally shows that the seven-year period was envisaged as operating on a fixed cycle which would have even further discouraged the making of a loan if the 'release' year was imminent. The likelihood of popular resistance to such measures with a consequent disregard for them is reflected in the injunctions . . . *do not be hard-hearted . . . Be open-handed* . . . In contrast the simple directness of the command of v. 11 expresses well the good intention behind the law. Israel's holiness was to be shown by its compassion for the poor. The definition of the right attitude required for living as God's people is memorable: *lend him on pledge as much as he needs* (v. 8).

The ruling highlights a recurrent feature of the Deuteronomic legislative rulings, and can be applied more widely in interpreting the biblical legislation. Good laws cannot be relied upon to work automatically, but call for a right attitude in their implementation. So there exists a need for a willingness to reach out beyond the law, as strictly formulated, to show compassion and mercy. The Old Testament is not a 'legalistic' literature in any such negative sense, but is consistently aware of those demands for justice and right-dealing which the law cannot by itself guarantee.

The release of slaves
15. 12–18

The ruling regarding the implementation of a special year of 'remission' leads naturally on to a further ruling regarding the release of slaves after the completion of their six-year term of servitude. There is an underlying connection since the major source of slaves was undoubtedly provided by those who fell into debt. Other sources were kidnapping (hence the prohibition of Exod. 21. 16) and prisoners taken in war (cf. Deut. 21. 10–14). The law here is a revision of that set out in Exod. 21. 2–6 which deals only with a male slave, whereas here the same ruling is applied to a female (v. 17). Marriage and probable motherhood were recognized as incurring a significantly different situation for a woman (cf. the ruling of Exod. 21. 7–11).

The injunction for an Israelite constantly to bear in mind the nation's origins in the slavery of Egypt becomes a consistent theme in Deuteronomy, establishing a reason for the adoption of a compassionate attitude towards victims of misfortune. That such human concern should sit side by side with the cruel rulings of Deut. 7. 2–6 and 13. 8 is both a disturbing and surprising aspect of the Deuteronomic legislation. The significant new feature of the ruling regarding the release of a slave after completion of the six-year term is to be seen in the injunction to provide such a person with the means to become an independent citizen with modest capital. Without such uncontracted support the granting of freedom would be an empty gesture. In this, and some other respects, the Deuteronomic legislation shows a stronger sensitivity to the realities of economic life than that found in the earlier Book of the Covenant. In doing so it offers a richer insight into the practical meaning of 'freedom'. Here therefore is to be seen a further insight into Deuteronomic awareness of the limitations of law, if implemented in a narrow legalistic fashion, and the importance of applying its rulings in a generous and compassionate manner.

The possibility that a slave might not wish to claim the right to freedom, but prefer to remain in the household of his, or her, master (vv. 16–17) follows the earlier ruling of Exod. 21. 5–6. There it is made clear that a slave contemplating release would have to forgo partner and family to do so. The Deuteronomic ruling reveals awareness that there could also be powerful economic arguments for forgoing the privilege of freedom and, as a result, accepting life in a permanent state of slavery. Certainly the deeply-fought issue of the ending of slavery throughout British dominions in the nineteenth century raised afresh consciousness of the necessary price of freedom which surfaces here. Freedom is never far removed from economic fairness.

The consecration of firstlings
15. 19–23

The last of the five units of this section returns to the basic underlying assumptions regarding holiness which appear in the ruling concerning tithes in 14. 22–27. The firstborn lambs and calves of livestock were to be slaughtered as a token of their consecration to God and not used for working, or, in the case of lambs, for the production of wool. Since God is the giver of all life, and is therefore ultimately the One who ensures the fertility of all creatures, it was right and proper that the firstborn of newly calving animals should be dedicated to God. This dedication would enable a celebratory meal to be held at the sanctuary involving the entire household (v. 20). So, in effect, it became a kind of thanksgiving meal for the fertility of the livestock, with the expectation that future offspring would then be blessed by God and would be available for normal use. The further proviso set out in v. 21 that offspring which showed any birth defect were not to be used for such a sacrificial meal illustrates the deeply felt rule, not only that God could not be 'cheated' in such fashion, but that what was defective in any way could not be made holy.

Throughout these rulings we discover a number of instructive aspects of the way in which Deuteronomy has developed and modified earlier rulings which have been retained and are still to be seen in the Book of the Covenant.

Most noteworthy is the extent to which the later Deuteronomic rulings take account of poverty in the community. This shows up in the implementation of the special 'third-year' tithe (14. 28–29), the concern to use the seven-year agricultural cycle to focus on a 'release' of debts (15. 2) and other measures for the alleviation of the misfortune of slaves and the poor.

Throughout there is a strong awareness that poverty creates a sharp dividing line in the community, challenging, and even undermining, the old ideal that Israel is a nation of brothers and sisters (15. 7). Although therefore Deuteronomy retains older sharply defined distinctions based on family and ethnic lines (cf. 14. 21, 29; 15. 3), it now reveals that, within its own inherited make-up, new social divisions have become apparent. Moreover these divisions also affected adversely the priestly community of the Levites, whose traditional role as sanctuary attendants was eroded by the restriction of offerings to one location. So Israel was becoming divided by economic distinctions, creating a gap between rich and poor which ought not to be there (cf. especially 15. 4, 6). What is relevant and valuable in looking at these rulings therefore, all of which have their roots in assumptions about the order of life and the calendar, which reach back far behind Deuteronomy, is their adaptation to take account of these economic changes. In no small measure Israel was becoming richer, but at the same time those who formulated these revised laws were fearful that it was becoming spiritually poorer. Measures, seemingly rather artificial in their rules, needed to be taken to stop the gap getting wider.

The festival calendar
16. 1–17

Issues regarding maintaining the holiness of God's name in the life of the community conclude with regulations setting out the instructions for the three primary religious festivals. The list in Deuteronomy represents a revision of two earlier lists which are preserved in Exod. 23. 14–19 (in 'the Book of the Covenant') and Exod. 34. 18–26 (the so-called 'Ritual Decalogue'). A still later and fuller list of the major festivals, ascribed by scholars to the post-exilic age, is given in Lev. 23. 1–44, further illustrating how central these festivals were to the religious life of the nation. Even so the pattern of Jewish religious festivals celebrated by New Testament times had been enlarged still more. The Deuteronomic list is a revision of what is presented earlier in Exodus 23 and 34 so that identifying and reflecting on the changes introduced is extremely instructive. The festivals are three in number.

The first is the Spring Festival, Passover and Unleavened Bread (vv. 1–8). The earlier calendars only refer to the eating of unleavened (unyeasted) bread for a period of seven days. It occurred in the month Abib (March–April) and was later fixed on the fourteenth–fifteenth days (Lev. 23. 4, 6). It belongs to the world of cereal farming, marking the end of the use of the previous season's crops and establishing an interval before the new season's yield began to be used for bread making. So it has its roots in the crop cycle of agriculture and the need for hygienic care. Here, however, it is linked to a historic moment in Israel's past when the saving power of God was especially evident (16. 3). This reinterpretation of the seven-day celebration made it into a prominent occasion for Israel's remembering God's past gracious acts to Israel as a nation. Worship was to be an opportunity for remembering that the entire nation was a community of people in covenant with God.

A new feature of this Deuteronomic ruling regarding the programme of the festival is the joining of the Unleavened Bread celebration with that of Passover. These are now brought together as two parts of one single event. That they were originally separate is indicated by the relevance of Passover to sheep farmers and Unleavened Bread to settled cereal farming – patterns of economy and life-style which were distinct and the occasion for rivalry and even open

71

conflict. Yet the fact that they both occurred in the Spring has served to bring them together. Passover involved the slaughter of a lamb and this action is interpreted in Exod. 12. 29–39 as a ritual of protection for the tents (and occupants) of the Israelites when God punished the Egyptians by killing all their firstborn children (Exod. 11. 4–7; 12. 29). The name is associated with a word meaning 'to hop, leap' and so has given rise to the 'passing over' of the Israelite tents.

With Deuteronomy the joining into one of the two festivals, and the conferring on this of a meaning directly tied to Israel's historic origins as a people delivered from slavery in Egypt, marks a new emphasis in Israel's festival calendar. No doubt the Spring occurrence served to encourage their being combined into a single celebration. An unexpected feature of the Deuteronomic instructions concerns the requirement that the Passover celebration take place at the central sanctuary (16. 5–8) and not in the various homes and villages of the citizens. Such a central celebration in Jerusalem is reported as having marked a unique feature of its revival in King Josiah's time (II Kgs. 23. 21–22). Yet it was evidently scarcely practicable to expect whole communities to be absent from home for so long a period so that later variations and concessions became essential. Nevertheless, as is evident in New Testament times, to attend the celebration of Passover in Jerusalem was a highly significant Jewish pilgrimage goal and doing so acquired popularity as the most distinctly Jewish religious festival.

The second of the celebrations is the Festival of Weeks, the prescription for this being set out in vv. 9–12. This was a festival celebrated seven weeks after the first cutting of the early harvest, requiring that an offering, commensurate with the crop-yield received (v. 10), be dedicated to God at the sanctuary. Lev. 23. 16 specifies that this is to take place on the fiftieth day after the sabbath following the offering of the first sheaf. From the Greek word for fiftieth this later became known as Pentecost. Once again the roots of the celebration in the seasons of agriculture are evident, but in later Jewish tradition it acquired additional meaning as an occasion for remembering God's gift of the law through Moses.

The third of the celebrations is the Festival of Booths (or Tabernacles) described in vv. 13–17. This was the last of the three mandatory festivals, requiring all menfolk to attend (cf. v. 16). The booths were roughly made temporary shelters, constructed from brushwood, in which the festival participants could sleep during the late summer period when the event took place. Since the same word

72

is used to describe the rough shelters made by soldiers living under campaign conditions they were associated with tents (or 'tabernacles'). The festival celebrated the end of harvest, especially the grape (wine) harvest and that of olives, so that it marked the close of the agricultural year. Deuteronomy does not make any direct link between these temporary shelters and the period of Israel's dwelling in tents during the journey through the wilderness although this is mentioned in the later calendar of Lev. 23. 43.

The Deuteronomic calendar of Israel's religious festivals marks the final group of regulations showing how the nation was to uphold the holiness of the name of the LORD in regard to the passing of time. As the weekly observance of the sabbath registered the division of time into weekly periods, so the three chief festivals extended this recognition across the year. In regard to the theological meaning and purpose of worship the linking of the seasonal Spring festivals with symbolism designed to assist the remembering of Israel's deliverance from the slavery of Egypt was a major step. It bears all the hallmarks of Deuteronomy's concern to ensure that worship was not simply an outward performance, however generous towards God and one's fellow-citizens in the offerings presented, but an inward act of recalling one's own spiritual identity. By participating in the preparation and festive rituals each worshipper would be led back to reflect on the nation's roots in gaining freedom from slavery by the unbought grace of the LORD God.

Further reflection on these festivals looks more broadly at the persistent Deuteronomic concern to ensure that the passage of time was marked by acts aimed at upholding the holiness of God's name. Keeping the sabbath as a day on which every citizen – even the slave and the disadvantaged alien – was entitled to rest and leisure, ensured that no human being's time could be wholly surrendered to the power of another. God had decreed otherwise from the very beginning of the world! Life required an ebb and flow of work and leisure, a rhythm of life which corresponded to inbuilt fundamental rhythms of the natural world. To despise and disregard these was to disregard the order of creation itself. How many of the most stressful and destructive illnesses of modern society result from the almost total erosion of the understanding that the management of time has a spiritual dimension?

The Appointment of Public Officials
16. 18–18. 22

A new section of the law code begins in 16. 18 and extends as far as 18. 22. It deals with various forms of public authority and administration, beginning with the appointment of judges to have oversight of the law. All told these authorized public servants fall into four categories, raising questions about their interrelationships with each other as much as about their own individual functions. These four categories are:

1) A class of officially appointed judges who are to be responsible for the just administration of the law (Deut. 16. 18–17. 13).
2) A king who is made subject to a number of restrictions aimed at preventing his exploitation of the people.
3) A class of levitical priests who are to be maintained by the offerings and firstfruit gifts of the people. Accordingly they are to have no separate land-holding within the community.
4) A series of charismatic prophets, who will appear from time to time and approve themselves by their spiritual integrity to stand in the tradition of Moses.

Such approved and recognized officials are to be carefully separated from association with any unapproved religious sanctuary or practice (16. 21–17. 7) and from soothsayers, diviners and the like, whose claims are rejected as wholly spurious and dangerous (18. 9–14). These four classes of public officials appear, at first glance, to be an ill-assorted group. Precisely how their separate authority might overlap or bring them into conflict with each other, and how such conflicts would be resolved are issues that are not spelled out. Nevertheless, when examined critically, several features stand out strikingly, giving rise to the claim that what is striven for is essentially a 'modern' social order, with authority spread across several groups, rather than one in which all power is channelled through one leader – the king.

An unexpected feature therefore is the modest role assigned to the king, who is effectively demoted from being the exalted, and divinely chosen, figure dispensing justice, military leadership and prosperity celebrated in the Psalms. Explicit limitations are laid down for the royal office, which itself is presented as a concession, rather than a

74

divinely ordained necessity for society. A third surprise comes in the authority given to prophets, who are sharply distinguished from spurious diviners and other semi-mystical practitioners, but who are, nevertheless, accorded a status no less than that of Moses himself (18. 18). They are presented as working alongside priests in serving the religious needs of the community.

How, in practice, these four groups would settle differences and avoid disputes where their authority overlapped is not made at all clear. The assumption appears to be that each group had its appropriate role to play in the community and that, together, they would generate necessary checks and balances to ensure a stable and fair social order. It appears that the deliberate demoting of the kingly office reflects the evident failure of Israel's kings to prevent exploitation of the people or achieve military security. Clearly kingship had been a cause of grievance ever since the days of King Solomon. The royal failure to uphold justice is well exemplified by Jeremiah's rebuke to King Jehoiakim for the self-indulgent building of a large palace and failure to ensure justice for the poor (Jer. 22. 13–17; cf. 22. 18 confirming the identity of the king as Jehoiakim). Wider dissatisfaction with the administrative leadership in Jerusalem, over which the king presided as head, is boldly spelt out in Isa. 5. 8–24. This prophetic levelling of royal pretensions cannot have been unique to a few individuals, but must undoubtedly have represented a widely felt dissatisfaction which is most clearly expressed in Samuel's catalogue of royal abuse in I Sam. 8. 10–18. It has led here to a rethinking of the role of necessary forms of public authority, with the law being set in foremost place.

From a wider socio-anthropological perspective we can discern that, throughout the days of Israel's monarchic rule, there had taken place a steady erosion of the authority of tribal chieftains in which clan elders and chiefs exercised power within the borders of the tribe. Kingship had gradually displaced this, but had been found wanting. Here in Deuteronomy, kingly rule is itself cut down in authority and set within a more broadly based structure of public offices.

The appointment of judges
    16. 18–20

The phrase *In every settlement . . . You must appoint for yourselves* (v. 18) raises vital questions, since it is not made clear who the 'You' are who are addressed. Throughout the ancient Near East kings were

75

undoubtedly chiefly those responsible for appointing an order of judges, and this may at one time have been the case in ancient Israel. Nevertheless Moses is said to have done so (cf. 1. 9–18; Exod. 18. 13–27) as one of the most significant of the social innovations ascribed to him. The lack of a fair and equal system of justice was a widespread social grievance voiced by the prophets. In earlier times justice was administered through tribal elders, who would have been respected local citizens, and Deuteronomy seems concerned to reinstate this policy.

The putting first of the setting up of a recognized order of officials responsible for the oversight of legal disputes and criminal justice shows clearly where the Deuteronomic authors placed their greatest emphasis for upholding public order (v. 19). This is where they saw their own role in the community and its priority is, in any case, implicit in their use of the lawbook form as a basis for a public policy document. This, in reality, covers all aspects of social and political, as well as more strictly legal, affairs. The prominence given to these officials shows a strong interest in legal expertise and also reveals the reason behind the authors' expectation of seeing the public implementation of their policies. So there is a positive belief that there would be strong public acceptance of them. The duties of these officials would be to keep records of cases and advise on procedures and punishments. To what extent they would serve as 'judges' in our modern sense is far from clear. They were to see that justice was done, with the people themselves accepting responsibility for the verdicts arrived at.

The Hebrew term used here for justice (*ṣedek*) in v. 20 is elsewhere often translated as 'righteousness'. In the conduct of lawsuits problems could arise where family links and influence were allowed to sway judgements, leaving members of weaker families and the marginalized sections of the community (widows, orphans, aliens) vulnerable. So even a term such as steadfast love (*ḥesed*) could hide an element of ambiguity if it was interpreted to imply love and loyalty primarily towards one's own family members, to the detriment of others. The Deuteronomic ruling is aware of the need for impartiality and spells out very forcibly the importance of interpreting the law without regard for the social standing of the parties concerned whether as accused or plaintiff. Bribes were clearly a frequent cause of influencing judicial activities, in which the commonplace giving and receiving of gifts to show respect could readily be distorted into a more openly corrupt practice (cf. Prov. 15. 27; 17. 8).

Laws against false worship
16. 21–17. 7

The introduction of three laws precluding the setting up of either a sacred pole (*Asherah*) or stone pillar (*Massebah*) at a rural shrine, or of offering defective animals to God as a sacrifice, comes surprisingly here (16. 21–17. 1). They appear out of place, since the regulations governing illicit sanctuaries and cult-objects belong with chapter 13. The explanation for their inclusion at this point is most probably to be found in the fact that they raise questions of religious loyalty which could have serious consequences, as is shown by the ruling in 17. 2–7. The law condemning anyone, whether man or woman, who breaks the first commandment by worshipping any deity other than, or alongside, the LORD God of Israel (17. 2–7) repeats what is set out earlier in 13. 6–11. Proven culprits were to face the death penalty (v. 5). The reason for the repetition here is most likely to be that such capital offences highlight cases where the principles of justice and fairness affirmed in 16. 20 could easily be infringed. The encouragement given in 13. 8 to inform on persons suspected of such offences, even members of one's own family, and against showing any compassion, could easily leave room for miscarriages of justice to occur. Throughout history legislation which has encouraged and rewarded informers for denouncing fellow citizens for offences against the state, or its official religion, has proved to be dangerously cruel and morally subversive.

The repetition in vv. 6–7 of the requirement that the normal laws of evidence relating to capital offences (cf. 19. 15) were to be maintained shows why the law regarding apostasy needed to be repeated. This safeguard had not been made sufficiently explicit in chapter 13 (cf. 13. 6, 12–14). Unscrupulous persons were not to be allowed to bring false accusations against innocent citizens without independent proof being brought by at least two witnesses (v. 6).

A religious court of appeal
17. 8–13

The likelihood of cases arising which could not be resolved by the normal legal safeguards regarding reliable evidence and trustworthy witnesses introduces in 17. 8–13 provision for a form of appeal court. Rather than allow such cases to lapse altogether they were to be referred to the levitical priests at the central sanctuary. Three typical situations requiring such referral are listed: *accidental or premeditated homicide, civil rights, or personal injury* (v. 8). The existence of such an appeal court shows that it was felt to be vitally important that a verdict of some kind was reached. This would serve to prevent disputes from developing into long-standing feuds and would help to compensate for the limitations of the laws of evidence.

The proposed order of judicial officials (v. 9) was clearly expected to be the primary and local basis for dealing first with cases. When these local officials were unable to do so then a more central court at the sanctuary could be called upon with the levitical priests from the sanctuary playing a part. These could, when necessary, make use of the sacred lot (Urim and Thummim). Clearly also a long-established convention regarded the priest as a fair-minded and independent assessor. In this way a decision of some kind would be arrived at to settle the issue (cf. Prov. 18. 18). The reference to *the judge who is in office in those days* must refer to the presiding figure of the council of lay judges mentioned later in 19. 17. Together with the designated priests these formed an appeal court responsible for deciding the most difficult cases in which new precedents might be established. The manner in which the Deuteronomic law code revises that of the earlier Book of the Covenant draws attention to the concerns which called for revised and amended judgements.

The priestly verdict was to be final and to allow no further appeal or argument (vv. 10–12). Disobeying it would be tantamount to disobeying God. In this manner the ultimate authority of the law was upheld, but through a joint decision between priests and the central judicial council. The divine origin and authority of law remained a primary principle.

Not only was the death penalty to be invoked if a plaintiff refused to accept the priest's verdict, but the reason for such a severe punishment is explained as a necessary public warning (v. 13). This ensured that the competence of the law to deal with serious problems of anti-social and criminal behaviour was not undermined by feuds and vigilante acts in which aggrieved citizens 'took the law into their own hands'.

The law of the king
17. 14–20

Deuteronomy is unique in the Pentateuchal legislation dealing with the constitution and polity of Israel in making provision for the installation of a king. In doing so it recognizes the historical fact that from the time of Moses to that of the election of king Saul Israel had had no king. So kingship is presented as a matter of concession and not of necessity. Moreover, the extended series of stories concerning how Israel had first introduced such a monarchy shows a comparable reserve which is taken by scholars to reflect the influence of the Deuteronomic viewpoint (I Sam. 8–12). When set over against the many psalm passages which celebrate with richly adulatory language the divine power and authority of the king (e.g. Pss. 2, 18, 20, 45), Deuteronomy's law appears surprisingly restrained.

The possibility that a foreigner might be king (v. 15) is surprising in that there is no firm indication that this was attempted. Nevertheless the hated Queen Jezebel was a Tyrian princess (I Kgs. 16. 31) and intermarriage between kings and royal princesses from neighbouring nations appears commonplace. Such actions cemented political alliances and also helped to sustain the mythological ideology that royal blood was a unique inheritance. When the Syrian–Israelite plot to depose King Ahaz in the time of the prophet Isaiah was mooted, there was a plan to install instead a certain 'son of Tabeal' (Isa. 7. 6). That he was of non-Davidic descent is most likely and possibly also of non-Israelite origin. The later Herodian family encountered opposition on account of their Idumean (Edomite) origins.

The example of king Solomon appears clearly to be in mind in the restrictions expressed in v. 16 (cf. I Kgs. 3. 1; 4. 26–28). The unmistakable allusions to the life-style of this ruler reflect directly the legacy of bitterness which his reign left. It had been directly responsible for the secession of the northern tribes from allegiance to the Davidic royal house (cf. 1 Kgs. 12. 16), and thus had been a primary cause of the break-up of Israel. The compromising nature of the narratives detailing Solomon's accession to the throne to succeed king David (I Kgs. 1–2), and details of the manner of his reign, further reveal the bitterness left by Solomon's legacy and the shadow it cast over kingship as a political institution. In reflecting this bitterness Deuteronomy endorses the possibility of a monarchy, but subjects it to strong, if rather unrealistic, safeguards.

Solomon was not the only Israelite ruler to have many wives (v. 17), although he was undoubtedly the best known. At this period polygamy was evidently widely practised and this fact enabled the author of Ecclesiastes to use the persona of Solomon to present a critical heart-searching reflection on the role of pleasure in the pursuit of human happiness (Eccles. 2. 1–23).

The entire strategy of Deuteronomy in outlining a polity for Israel's future rests on the fundamental conviction that it was Moses and the gift of a book of divine law, not kingship, with its principle of dynastic rule, that represented God's will for the government of the nation (v. 18). The mythological background to the ancient belief in the divine right of kings to rule on earth is clearly shown in Ps. 2. 7. Deuteronomy has 'demythologized' altogether such a belief in the divinity of kings and replaced it with a reasoned constitutional alternative. The king was to be subject to the authority of the book of the law given through Moses and this commitment to the law is enjoined upon Solomon by no less a figure than king David himself (cf. I Kgs. 2. 1–4). No citizen, not even the king, could be above the law of God. By this rule an important building stone was set in place for the architecture of political power within the nation. Final authority was to be vested in a historic 'charter' of national life, rather than in the arbitrary control of one individual.

Deuteronomy's critical estimate of the monarchy (v. 20) reflects feelings that had been long present within Israelite national life. Not even David had been above criticism. Yet Deuteronomy's negative assessment may also take some account of the disaster of 587 BCE which put an end to the continuance of the rule of the Davidic dynasty in Jerusalem. Jehoiachin, the deposed king, was taken into exile in Babylon along with his family and the prophet Jeremiah saw no future for them (cf. Jer. 22. 24–30). However another faction within the defeated nation kept alive the hope that descendants of this royal house would one day return to the throne in Jerusalem (cf. II Kgs. 25. 24–27; Jer. 33. 14–26; I Chron. 3. 17–24).

The levitical priests
    18. 1–8

After law officers and kings, the third order of public officials who were to hold responsibility for the government of Israel is the levitical priesthood. Deuteronomy's ruling is important for what it implies regarding the status of Levites and the manner of their support. It affirms the right of 'the whole tribe of Levi' to serve as priests, in contrast to the different portrayal presented in Num. 3–4; 18. 1–7. This is usually ascribed by scholars to the later (post-exilic) Priestly stratum of instructions contained in the Pentateuch and assigns only lesser duties to the Levites, reserving priestly service for descendants of Aaron alone. It is evident from the narrative records that in earlier times not all Israel's priests had been Levites since some of David's sons were appointed to be such (II Sam. 8. 18). Deuteronomy's ruling represents a middle stage in the development of priestly organization. The lack of any territorial inheritance for the Levites (v. 2) appears as a primary reason for their impoverished state. They seem wholly dependent on the people's gifts of tithes whereas in Num. 35. 1–8; Jos. 21 no less than forty-eight cities are allocated to them. Yet this information most probably belongs to the later (Priestly) tradition. The law concerning the single sanctuary was clearly seen to bring far-reaching consequences for the Levites, putting them in need of special support. The tithe revenues due to the Levites are set out in 14. 27–29 (cf. also 16. 11, 14). Further detailed rules are given in Num. 18. 21–28 reflecting the later (Priestly) viewpoint. These appear more generous than those laid down in Deuteronomy.

That Levites would be living in various towns widely dispersed throughout the nation is recognized in v. 6. Their reputation for religious integrity, to the point of ruthlessness, in maintaining loyalty to the LORD God is reflected in Exod 32. 25–29; cf. also Deut. 33. 9. Deuteronomy's concern for the Levites has suggested to some that they may have been among the book's authors, but their impoverished condition makes this unlikely. It was their reputation for religious loyalty, rather than their priestly activities, which made them a primary focus for Deuteronomy's concern.

The ruling concerning the freedom of all Levites to serve as priests (v. 7) is significant in that it recognizes that not all Levites had been servants of the one central sanctuary in Jerusalem. Some are likely to have been priests in other towns and it is plausible that many had been deprived of their priestly role as a result of the political turmoil that befell the Northern Kingdom of Israel under the harsh terms of Assyrian control following Samaria's fall to that imperial power in 722 BCE. Deuteronomy's ruling looks to the situation that would inevitably arise as a consequence of the restriction of offering sacrificial gifts to one central sanctuary. Surprisingly II Kgs. 23. 9 reports that the privilege of service at the central sanctuary affirmed here was not conceded.

There is some uncertainty concerning how the Levites would have family property to sell (18. 8) since they were to have no inheritance. The inference appears to be that no account was to be taken of any inherited property, drawn from family links, when considering the entitlement to serve at the central sanctuary.

From a historical point of view the Deuteronomic ruling concerning the Levites has a major bearing on the history of Israel's priesthood, outlining a situation which was recognized to be substantially new as a result of the restriction of worship and the offering of tithes to one sanctuary only. From the preacher's perspective it raises a different set of questions. Throughout much of Christian history the Old Testament rules concerning tithes and their use to support a priestly order have been appealed to in order to affirm fundamental principles concerning economic support for the Church and its ministers. The broad principle that this should derive from the gifts of the many, not the patronage of a few, has been important. At times tithes have been legally demanded and have consequently been felt to be an oppressive Church 'tax', which has been greatly resented. Yet less controversially the voluntary giving of tithes enshrines a spiritual principle. In Deuteronomy what is envisaged is not that the Levites should become a wealthy and powerful order, as frequently was the case in antiquity where priests sometimes came to exercise great power, even becoming king-makers. Rather they were to be supported so as to share fully and equally in the life, festivities and general well-being of the community as a whole. Their loyalty and commitment to the LORD God was to be enabled and rewarded.

True and false prophets
18. 9–22

A primary feature of the religious life of all the communities of the ancient Near East consisted of various forms of mantic, or soothsaying, activity. Most familiar here are the prophets and prophetesses who are referred to in the Old Testament who simply spoke as the mouthpieces of a god or goddess. Yet they were merely one type, or branch, of such activity, some forms of which were mechanistic and closely tied to a sanctuary, whereas other such practitioners were freelance and deliverers of oracles and interpreters of dreams. The different activities were given different titles, depending on the type of oracle-giving which they pursued. Interpreting 'signs' on the markings of animals, or the patterns of oil on water – even shooting arrows into the air (cf. Ezek. 21. 21) – all formed part of these activities. Straightforward prophetic speech was the most popular, but even this could contain mysterious cryptic utterances not unlike riddles. A very popular form of such oracle-giving was by the interpretation of dreams, besides various signs relating to recovery from illness (cf. Isa. 38. 21–22; in REB the verse is transposed to follow v. 6) all of which

82

became part of this many-sided activity. That it could be dangerous in generating alarm and fear, and led to the belief that the most expert of such practitioners could cast spells and induce sickness, or even death, was recognized.

It is in this regard that we can understand the inclusion of a law in the Book of the Covenant which condemned to death a woman found practising such sorcery (Exod. 22. 18). Deuteronomy's law prohibiting these activities (18. 9–14) has certainly been developed from this but has then been further elaborated to accord an authorised place to approved prophetic individuals (18. 15–22).

Already Deuteronomy has sought to preclude the activities of prophets and the like who plied their trade in the name of some other deity than that of the LORD God of Israel (13. 1–5). The concern in this section was to prevent the operation of men or women who made use of whatever divine name was acceptable, but who, nonetheless, engaged in undesirable and threatening actions which were believed capable of harming members of the community. A particular instance that is outlawed is that of making a child 'pass through fire' (v. 10). Precisely what cruel rite is implied by this is unclear. It may have been no more than a barbaric kind of infanticide. However more than this is implied by the reference to the practice of infant sacrifices in II Kgs. 23. 10. Burials from Phoenician settlements in several of the Mediterranean lands have provided evidence of large numbers of funeral urns containing infants' bones, supporting such a gruesome conclusion. The linking of such a ritual with the name Moloch (II Kgs. 23. 10) has given rise to the suggestion that the passage through fire was linked to some form of votive rite.

All told the variety of forms of divination and soothsaying covered a range of claims to foresee the future, some of which were rather simplistic. However, the catalogue also included persons who claimed to have the ability, either in a trance, or with the aid of various objects, to speak on behalf of figures from a supernatural realm, including ghosts from the past (v. 11). Such a conjuring up of a dead leader is described in detail in regard to king Saul (I Sam. 28. 3–25).

Since the various types of necromancer, dream interpreter and soothsayer, including prophets, appear largely to have been self-appointed, it is evident that their existence could not easily be restrained, except by a policy of education and public rebuke, with threats of more severe punishment for cases of sorcery.

The injunction in v. 13 for Israel to be *undivided in your service* to the LORD God (NRSV reads 'completely loyal') uses the adjective 'perfect,

83

blameless' which is the Hebrew term used to denote an approved sacrificial animal (cf. Exod. 12. 5). In the later biblical tradition it is employed to denote right conduct (cf. Gen. 6. 9; Ps. 18. 23, 25) and, in this sense, it underlies the Greek adjective for 'perfect' in Matt. 5. 48.

In spite of all such warnings it is evident that, in regard to matters of health and childbirth, there was a continuing temptation for individuals to resort privately to such practitioners, and it is this temptation that v. 14 sought to discourage.

Against these dangerous religious activities Deuteronomy sought to affirm a positive and responsible place to true prophets who fulfilled their tasks in total commitment to the LORD God of Israel. These persons fulfilled, in the mind of the Deuteronomic authors, a vital and necessary role in national life. At the highest level they included the major figures of Elijah and Elisha who had fought vigorously for total loyalty to the historical religious allegiance of Israel. These figures were regarded as fulfilling a role within the national life comparable to that of Moses himself (v. 15; cf. 34. 10). Within the ongoing course of national development, new challenges would be faced and crises would have to be overcome. In such situations prophets were important, and it is noteworthy that in II Kgs. 17. 13–14, the primary task that they fulfilled is regarded as that of calling the nation back to its Mosaic foundations.

Since God could not, and would not, speak directly to the people, the divine truth could only be conveyed through a human voice (vv. 16–18). So prophets were necessary, even though their charismatic and individual status made them a form of spiritual leadership which was difficult to control, and which could lead to difficulties and disloyalty. Deuteronomy gives qualified approval therefore to prophets who would arise from time to time. By this phrase the ruling is not affirming the existence of a fixed succession of 'official prophets' who would continue in an unbroken line to continue the leadership of Moses, but rather is pointing to their occasional intermittent appearance. Their spontaneity and ability to speak from God directly on contemporary issues was important and necessary. But their work could only be approved and acted upon, when all such prophets showed themselves to be loyal to the laws and traditions of Moses himself. He alone was the greatest of all the prophets (34. 10) who had established a tradition of truth and obedience which could never be set aside.

The case of false prophets had consistently shown itself able to create difficulties, since no formal and outward test could distinguish

84

true from false when each prophet claimed to have received God's message. Those who misled the nation by presuming to speak in the name of some god other than the LORD would easily reveal their true colours. To worship other gods has already been outlawed in 13. 1–5. More difficult were cases where no such blatant disloyalty was displayed and where conflicting messages were given by different prophets.

Jeremiah's confrontation with the false prophet Hananiah (Jer. 28–29) represents a near-classical disclosure of the problem that false prophets brought. Telling people what they wanted to hear made the prophet Hananiah popular, but simply confirmed his worthlessness. Yet how could this be recognized at the time? The narrator of the incident sets out the criterion that true prophets had consistently forewarned Israel of war and other disasters, whereas the false prophets had consistently promised only peace (Jer. 28. 7–9). Such a simple guideline is strongly Deuteronomic in its admonitory tone, but also leaves a forbidding picture of prophetic activity which allows too little room for messages of hope.

From the modern preacher's perspective the introduction of the subject of the authority and truthfulness of prophets and prophecy is of considerable value in dealing with a problem which continues to face most forms of organized religion. Christian faith leans heavily on tradition and on the truths contained within the Bible and creeds. Yet such can readily become sterile and rigid, calling for a renewal of spirit and relevant insight to deal with contemporary issues. So the stimulus offered by powerful new charismatic teachers is needed to awaken fresh zeal and commitment. All too often, however, among such worthy new leaders powerful voices emerge teaching dangerous novelties and gaining a ready following. Ultimately they lead to disaster, as recent examples reveal. The biblical response to this danger is not to deny the need for new prophetic leadership, but to ensure that it conforms to the established tradition, which Deuteronomy interprets to lie in the spirit of Moses.

85

Laws of life and death
19. 1–21. 23

Capital offences and warfare
19. 1–13

After establishing the roles of the four main classes of officials responsible for public administration, the law code turns in 19. 1–21. 19 to deal with issues which relate to the taking of human life. The first section in 19. 1–13 deals with the setting aside of three cities which are to provide centres for dealing with cases of suspected murder. The last unit in 21. 1–9 makes provision for the situation in which a corpse has been found and a murder suspected, but the killer unknown. Overall these provisions come under the umbrella of the commandment 'You shall not murder' (Deut. 5. 17). The exception appears to be the law in 19. 14 prohibiting the removal of a neighbour's landmark, but a reason for its inclusion at this point may be discerned.

Beginning with 19. 1–2 the law code provides for the setting aside of three cities where cases of homicide could be subjected to authorized legal investigation. In this way a fair trial by competent officials could be set up. The provision is additional to the three cities situated east of the River Jordan already designated for such a purpose in 4. 41–43. The basic provision is then extended further in 19. 8–10 to allow for three other locations to be added, possibly intending those referred to in chapter 4. In Num. 35. 6, 11 such locations are called 'cities of refuge'. The ruling presumes that Israel's legal jurisdiction extended over a wide area, and was aimed at ensuring that, after a death had occurred, no one fleeing from an avenger had too great a distance to travel.

The primary purpose of the specially designated cities is explained (vv. 4–7) as providing a temporary refuge for any person involved in the killing of another. The need to distinguish between cases of deliberate murder and those of accidental manslaughter was paramount (cf. Exod. 21. 12–14). Difficulties arose on two fronts. Primarily the need was for time in which independent investigators could examine what had happened, before any avenger took premature action against an accused person. Time was needed to call relevant witnesses to find out whether the person accused of killing another had intended to kill.

The long-standing convention that allowed an 'avenger of blood' to

86

take revenge for any killing was a deeply embedded feature of the old tribal and clan system. It had its roots in the assumption that responsibility for justice rested with the family chiefs who protected the interests of the large extended family, or clan. In such circumstances vengeance could be swiftly exacted with little regard for impartiality. The care with which Deuteronomy's ruling spells out that a person guilty of accidental killing was not to be punished as a murderer (v. 10) shows the importance attached to an individual's intention. The law had to protect the innocent as well as punish the guilty so that the deeply felt concern to avoid 'bloodguilt' resting on the community was no taboo-based scruple, but a matter of reason and intent. In this concern Jesus faithfully interprets the spirit of the ancient law in Matt. 5. 21–22.

The practicability of enforcing a system of legal administration which called for proper investigation of criminal actions in the community, depended for its efficacy upon an authorized body of accredited officials. We have earlier encountered two classes of such officials in the persons of judges (16. 18) and priests (17. 9). We now meet a further group in the city elders who are mentioned in v. 12. They were presumably respected local heads of families who took responsibility for order in their town or city. It was never the purpose of the provision of the cities to provide a way of escape from justice for a person involved in another's death. Rather it was to make sure that justice was done within the scope of the law insofar as this was practicable.

The provision of these cities has sometimes been regarded as Deuteronomy's attempt to provide a secular alternative to the very ancient idea that a killer could find refuge in a sanctuary (cf. Joab in I Kgs. 2. 28–35). By the restriction to one single sanctuary Deuteronomy had limited the possibilities for this to offer a basis for help. However, it appears more likely that both traditions of temporary protection were ancient and ran in parallel with each other. The new situation which Deuteronomy demands brought a change of emphasis, with the priesthood being called upon in matters of justice only as a court of final appeal.

There is much in Deuteronomy which is secular in its design and we find its lawmakers deeply committed to furthering the cause of justice through fair and recognized procedures in which the whole community is involved. Law called for experience and discernment and its officials had to contend with the powerful influence of tribal and family kin-groups who could use their power unjustly. The deep-

87

rooted popular suspicion of the corruptibility of justice is a frequent complaint of the prophets (e.g. Amos 5. 7–13). Deuteronomy strove for real justice, based on God's supreme fairness, administered with impartiality, but it also had to recognize that laws could often be limited in their effectiveness.

When seen in homiletical perspective the provision of the cities of refuge may appear to stand at the edge of biblical concern with justice and the human situation as we experience it today. Yet their establishment bears witness to two very important aspects of human social order. Of primary importance in Christian tradition is the fact that their very existence testifies to the recognition that it is the attitude of heart and mind, not simply outward acts, that lies at the very heart of morality. Accidents can happen in which human life is lost, with no one person being expressly blameworthy, as the example of 19. 5 illustrates. Furthermore, even the most even-tempered and well-intentioned person can be provoked and angered to the point in which unnecessary and unaccustomed violence occurs (Matt. 5. 21–26). An accidental death can trigger feelings of hatred and a desire for revenge that, in retrospect, are not justified. So the provision of time and place for passions to cool and impartial investigation to take place was a major step in advancing the cause of justice for all. There is in fact a very direct path from the provision of these cities where motives could be examined after a death had occurred and the teaching of Jesus in the Sermon on the Mount.

Laws of evidence
   19. 14–21

That the moving of a neighbour's landmark (v. 14) could prove a deeply rooted problem, resulting in the misappropriation of another person's land, is shown by the frequent biblical references to it; cf. Prov. 22. 28; 23. 10 and Deut. 27. 17. It was a serious misdemeanour against which it was very difficult to implement effective legislation on account of the lack of maps and the inexactness of descriptions of territory. The reason for the inclusion of the law at this point at first appears unclear, but it is almost certainly because it highlights an offence where proof of guilt was difficult to establish. It introduces an issue which focuses on matters of principle concerning rules of evidence since it was a prime example of a case calling for great care on this front. The rulings that follow concern admissible and inadmissible evidence.

The question of evidence, taken on oath, is central to legal proceedings and already the ninth commandment rules against 'baseless evidence'. The well-nigh classic instance of the killing of Naboth as a consequence of royal lies is set out in I Kgs. 21. 1–24. The law governing the admissibility of evidence to substantiate a charge (v. 15) appears originally to have been devised to apply to cases involving the death penalty. Any miscarriage of justice in a charge of murder had the most dire consequences. However, once the principle was recognized that a single witness could not be relied upon, and could even be acting out of malicious intent, the issues raised needed to be applied more widely. These principles were valid for all legal cases, as we have already noted in respect of charges of religious apostasy (17. 6). Accordingly the important feature here is that the principle is applied to cases for *any crime* or wrongdoing. Two witnesses were a minimum, but three were desirable.

The problems created by a malicious witness were serious, not simply because they could lead to the wrongful punishment of an innocent person, but because their activities threatened to undermine the whole apparatus of legal administration (vv. 16–21). Accordingly serious punishment had to be meted out to a person who committed perjury. Furthermore, both in the emphasis placed on such offences in the Ten Commandments and in the repeated condemnation in wisdom sayings of those who went about as slanderers dispensing malicious gossip, it was recognized that offenders might often be hard to bring to trial.

The reference in v. 17 to 'two parties' implies a situation in which two witnesses presented conflicting evidence which made a case unresolvable. It then required that these witnesses be brought before God at the sanctuary. They and their evidence were then to be examined by the priests and judges, who could administer solemn oaths, in line with the appeals procedure outlined in 17. 8–13 (cf. also Exod. 22. 11). The 'careful examination' of v. 18 allowed for the calling of other witnesses to establish the credentials of the suspect witnesses. Evidently a particular concern was the need to prevent anyone acting as a supporting witness in cases when their evidence was not truly independent. Such swearing of an oath to a statement which was not known to be true would have been included under the broad prohibition of the third commandment (Deut. 5. 11; cf. also Matt. 5. 33–37).

The declaration *You must rid yourselves of this wickedness* (v. 19; NRSV: 'So you shall purge the evil from your midst') is applied to

89

activities which threatened the very basis of community life. Some cases of perjury might appear to be of marginal importance, but they undermined the integrity of the whole judicial system and therefore were dealt with severely. The warning of v. 20 closely resembles that of 17. 13 where it concerns the imposition of the death penalty on any person who refused to accept a verdict given by the priest. The threatening intention of the rule reflects the deep awareness that perjury might be difficult to prove and so those who were found to be guilty of such an offence had to be made into examples to discourage others.

Finally the stereotyped phrasing setting out the so-called *lex talionis* (v. 21) – the law of vengeance – demanded an equivalent retribution for the wrong that would have been brought upon another by the malicious accusation. The formula, with variations in its wording, is used in two other instances in the Old Testament, particularly in regard to brawling which led to personal injury (Exod. 21. 23–25; Lev. 24. 18–20). In each instance it is evidently a citation of a forcefully worded, and deeply felt, principle of justice. Violence leading to injury created an imbalance in relationships which had to be put right by inflicting an equivalent hurt upon the wrongdoer. The principle is quite widely reflected in ancient Babylonian and Assyrian legislation, but rather less so in the Old Testament. In certain situations compensation, rather than retributive maiming, could be made when injury had been inflicted upon a slave (Exod. 21. 26–27). Although easily memorized, and usefully voicing a principle of equality of justice, it is far from being a pervasive principle of biblical laws. The maintenance of community wholeness and peace, giving rise to the concern to achieve a verdict whenever possible, is a far more widely felt feature of Old Testament legislation.

Although the Old Testament *torah* is described as a book of 'law' it contains far less in the way of legislation for the adminstration of public justice than is often supposed. This is because a just and fulfilled society requires more than laws in order to establish goodness and virtue. It is this seeking of a larger goal for the good life that makes the biblical ideas of wholehearted and sincere love of God and of fellow human beings so important. Much that has proved most enduring in the Deuteronomic legislation rests on its appeal for a right attitude and a heart-searching personal integrity. In this regard it establishes a path of insight into moral and social evil which is developed more fully, rather than countermanded, in the Sermon on the Mount.

Laws are necessary since they protect society from arbitrary violence and serve to uphold justice and welfare which provide a foundation for a healthy quality of life. Yet laws alone are not enough. Deuteronomy is well aware of this and recognizes that laws have their limitations by reminding the reader of the necessity for maintaining a right attitude of compassion towards slaves and the impoverished. It is also aware that the administration of law could run into serious problems and could be abused by false accusations and perjury. Truth was a vital element of the satisfactory pursuit of justice. Against such abuse the priests of the sanctuary provided an important back-up for what the unaided lawcourt could not achieve.

Concessions and restrictions in time of war
20. 1–9

A significant feature of Deuteronomy's laws lies in the inclusion of several which concern conduct in time of war, even to the point of establishing rules for offering terms of surrender to an enemy. Throughout the Hebrew Bible the practice of warfare is accepted as an inevitable part of the human situation. At a number of points warfare is viewed as a divine activity, with God leading the people into battle, and even teaching prowess in military skills (cf. Ps. 18. 34). At other times, more particularly in the prophetic writings, war is regarded as evil and destructive, so that a coming time of world peace when all warfare has been ended is eagerly awaited (cf. Isa. 2. 2–4; 54. 11–17). For the most part Deuteronomy accepts the inevitability of warfare and establishes certain goals for it and limitations to it. Its primary goal is seen as the acquisition of territory, especially the territory that was claimed as promised to Israel's patriarchal ancestors and conquered under Joshua's leadership. In this case God gives assurance of victory, on condition that certain personal restraints and attitudes are adopted.

The 'rules of warfare' in Deuteronomy have frequently been described as constituting a charter for 'Holy War', but this is a rather erroneous designation. Since warfare necessarily involved the shedding of blood, then, on this account, certain limitations were also involved, otherwise the principle of the Noachic warning (Gen. 9. 6) would apply and bloodguilt would follow. War had to be conducted in a manner so that its permitted goals could be secured without unnecessary bloodshed, and without bringing bloodguilt on the participants – which could occur even when they had been victorious in battle. So warfare was hedged around with scruples since its conduct impinged on the realm of holiness (cf. Joel 3. 9 where soldiers are bidden to prepare for battle with the command: 'sanctify a war', cf. NRSV margin). To the modern reader the notion that war can achieve a holy purpose appears wholly unacceptable. Deuteronomy's rules of war appear to have been put together from a variety of traditions and sources and, in spite of the claims of some scholars, do not add up to a clear and consistent set of rules for the conduct of 'a holy war'. In general they display a surprisingly theoretical character.

The opening scenario of how a battle situation would take place (v. 1) recognizes that Israel would have to field a conscript army which would be faced by forces with superior equipment and greater numbers than it could hope to match. This had certainly been the experience when Israel had succumbed repeatedly to the large, professionally organized, armies of Assyria and Babylon which had reduced the once extensive territory ruled by David to a wilderness of ruination and defeat. From a military perspective it is evident that the relatively small kingdom of Israel had had no serious prospect of stemming the incursions of the 'super powers' of Egypt and Mesopotamia. Hope of effective resistance lay in forming multi-national alliances between the smaller powers that lay between them. But these proved insufficient and impossible to maintain. That Israel could enlist only a conscript army contrasted with the professional fighting forces of the ancient Great Powers.

The role of the priest in presenting a morale-boosting speech (vv. 2–4) must certainly reflect actual practice from the past. The Deuteronomic accounts of how Moses and Joshua had been successful in their military campaigns places great weight on the role of faith and high morale as a necessary precondition of victory. Deuteronomy's rhetorical skill was well suited to such speech-making and a classic example of its central theme is placed on the lips of David in his challenge to Goliath (I Sam. 17. 45–47).

The mention of 'officials' in vv. 5–7 indicates regional appointees who served as marshals to ensure that those eligible for military service fulfilled their duty. The concessions offered to those who were entitled to exemption focus on the need for ensuring that the present generation of Israelites would be protected in order to build the future nation.

The prominent emphasis given to high morale as a necessary condition of military service (v. 8) reflects a distinctive Deuteronomic

92

understanding of the nature of warfare. The link between trust in the power of the LORD God to give victory and courage in battle is noteworthy and is allied to Deuteronomy's concern to counter any spirit of despair and disillusionment to which the reader may succumb.

Conditions for offering terms of surrender
20. 10–18

The cruel and devastating consequences of war are well reflected in many passages of the Old Testament, especially in prophecies anticipating the imminent arrival of invading armies, or the slaughter of battle followed by famine. Deuteronomy recognizes both the cruelty and pity of war, but justifies it as a necessary means to claiming Israel's divinely promised territory. Nevertheless the book offers some modest concessions towards averting unnecessary loss of life (vv. 10–14).

Walled cities provided the chief basis of defence against military attack, so that the breaking of the siege defences of a city formed the primary strategy of offensive warfare. Assyrian success in devising tactics to achieve such break-throughs had been a major feature of its growth in power and had exposed Israel's vulnerability. Deuteronomy's portrayal of military operations clearly reflects awareness of these tactics. Terms of peace were to be offered to cities under attack, but only at the price of surrender to slavery. The threat of the imposition of humiliating conditions of surrender is presented as a leading factor in elevating Saul to summon Israel to fight, and, after gaining victory, to claim kingship over the nation (cf. I Sam. 11. 1–15).

The ruling that, once a city was conquered, all its menfolk should be killed (v. 13) was exceptionally harsh. The wall-reliefs fashioned to celebrate Sennacherib's conquest of Lachish in 701 BCE illustrate with terrifying clarity the cruelty of such slaughter. Babylonian action after the capture of Jerusalem in 598 BCE appears to have been less vindictive since it resulted in the rounding up and forcible deportation to Babylonia of a large number of male prisoners. The final surrender terms when a siege collapsed were negotiable. In Deut. 2. 34 it is reported that, after the defeat of Sihon of Heshbon, men, women and children were slaughtered and only the livestock kept as spoil.

The harsher treatment demanded for the survivors of cities closer to Israel's homeland (vv. 15–18) is introduced in order to satisfy the religious demand that the persons and property of all the former inhabitants of Israel's land be destroyed; cf. Deut. 7. 2. The reason for

93

making this distinction was therefore purely religious. Throughout this group of laws there is an awareness that the rigid application of basic principles could point to conflicting rules between one line of action and another. The need for establishing priorities was therefore an important feature of legal development.

The justification for this policy of total destruction is presented in v. 18 as a need to remove all vestiges of the religious life of these former inhabitants. Israelites would not then be tempted to emulate them. Had such a destructive policy been followed in Israel's occupation of the land, these repeated denunciations by Deuteronomy of earlier religious practices would scarcely have been necessary – a conclusion which strongly indicates that they were still prevalent, and even popular. A return to the religious and cultural life of the older population of the land was what Deuteronomy most feared, threatening the loss of central (Jerusalem) authority and its power to unify the remnants of the nation. The inclusion of these rules of warfare appears surprisingly unrealistic, but is in agreement with the claim that, when complete loyalty to the LORD God was present, victory would be assured even against an overwhelmingly superior enemy.

The wider concern for the productivity and welfare of the land (v. 19) points to an awareness of the close dependence of human beings on the natural world for food and building resources. The authors were also fully aware of the immense devastation brought to Israel's cultivated land by the military campaigns waged from Assyria and Babylonia. These had long-term consequences on the land's productivity, bringing years of famine (cf. Ezek. 5. 12). A prolonged siege not only brought with it the neglect and plundering of fertile land, but also led to deliberate actions to render good land infertile as a punitive measure (cf. Deut. 29. 22–23).

Timber was needed for battering-rams in the breaking of a siege (v. 20), and was used to make siege-engines, resembling large wooden shields, which enabled attacking forces to approach and gain a foothold on a city wall. Such techniques of siege-breaking are well illustrated in the Sennacherib wall-reliefs of the attack on Lachish.

The problem of unsolved murder
21. 1–9

The series of laws dealing with cases involving death concludes with a ritual procedure for dealing with situations in which a murder victim is found but no culprit can be traced. It is a mixture of sacral

94

and legal procedures designed to remove any stain of bloodguilt from contaminating the land which would hinder its life-giving power. It also ensured that adequate notice was taken of the fact that a crime had taken place but the circumstances precluded that the culprit could be found and punished. That the corpse is found lying in open country (v. 1) implies that there were no witnesses to the assault. Furthermore the need to ascertain the nearest town (v. 2) strongly suggests that the victim may be unidentified, but, whether the victim were known or not, the significant point is that no culprit was traceable. The murdered corpse defiled the land, and so this had to be cleansed of the harmful consequence of bloodguilt, taking full account of the inability to proceed with a formal legal case. The elders of the nearest town are those primarily involved and the 'judges' (Samaritan text reads 'officers') appear as observers who would have to agree that there was insufficient evidence on which to proceed and bring charges. Once they had confirmed that this was so the elders could go ahead with the ritual to remove the defilement of the land.

The procedure that follows is to slaughter a heifer, effectively as a kind of substitute for the untraceable murderer (vv. 3–4). The fact that the heifer had never been used for work and that the ritual was required to be carried out on uncultivated land were important as part of the concern to ensure that death (the unavenged murder victim) and life (the fertility of the soil) were not mixed together. The heifer was then killed by the elders, making it, rather than the unidentified murderer, the bearer of the necessary punishment. Every death needed to be avenged, which was achieved in this instance by using an animal substitute for the murderer. The presence of the priests (v. 5) was necessary since the declaration of innocence by the town elders took place as a solemn oath before God. In effect they were declaring that they, and their township, had done what was possible to avenge the crime. By making a public avowal of their own, and their town's, innocence (vv. 6–8) they were making a public declaration that no prosecution could be brought. The right and duty of the law to punish was upheld, but was left in abeyance when no culprit could be brought to trial. The appeal to God to 'absolve' the people generally for responsibility of the crime uses the verb otherwise employed to indicate atonement. Hence REB reads: *Accept expiation, O* LORD . . . (NIV 'Accept this atonement . . .').

Finally the formula *you will rid yourselves of the guilt of innocent blood* (v. 9) marks an instructive combination of sacral (holiness) rules aimed at preventing an untimely death from polluting the land, there-

95

by rendering it infertile, and legal concerns, designed to prevent negligence leading to failure to apprehend and prosecute a murderer.

Throughout the laws dealing with murder, manslaughter and other offences involving the possibility of capital punishment there is a significant bringing together of concerns with the nature of justice. On one hand there is a residual awareness that, at the very heart of popular understanding of natural justice, there lies a belief that it ought to 'make the punishment fit the crime'. Accordingly the principle of retribution is cited poetically in 19. 20. Punishment ought to be 'tit for tat'! Interwoven with this principle is the even older taboo-laden belief that the shedding of blood was an affront to God, the ultimate giver of life, and therefore brought harm to the community. So unatoned killing could pollute the land – a principle openly expressed in the appended rule in 21. 23. The demand for careful weighing of evidence and cross-examination of witnesses in cases of homicide has been extended more widely to establish 'rules of evidence' applicable to other cases also.

Seen in the light of modern concerns with justice, popular revulsion against certain crimes, and even failure to apprehend the culprits, this strange-sounding biblical law has a number of instructive features. The idea of retribution – life for life – is a principle often quoted in defence of capital punishment even today. Yet it immediately raises some of the most complex and far-reaching issues concerning the establishing of justice. It is undeniable that the processes of law are not infallible and a person once executed in error, cannot be restored to life. Moreover murder is not always the result of a clear-cut case of intent to kill. Accidents can happen, tempers can flare up, and brawls can get out of hand, so that one person's death may not be solely the responsibility of one culpable murderer. It may have been accidental, or the victim may share some of the blame. So the context in which the crime occurred has to be examined carefully.

We find permeating these laws signs of careful reflection on the nature of justice and the responsibility of a legal system. The old tribal custom of leaving punishment to the victim's family was not a fair and trustworthy option. Yet, in the desire to replace this age-old tradition of exacting vengeance by more formal legal action, too hasty an emphasis on apprehending and punishing the accused person could lead to innocent citizens being wrongly punished. A comparable anxiety to allay public anger and disquiet has certainly been the reason for some glaring miscarriages of justice in Great Britain in recent years. The desire to see justice done may override the caution necessary to ensure that the innocent are protected. The complex nature of many crimes of violence has to be taken fully into account, with due regard for where the blame lies. At the same time simply ignoring violent crime is wholly undesirable so that letting cases drop for lack of evidence has to be avoided if at all possible. Since it is the duty of the law to protect the innocent as well as to punish the guilty, reliable and flexible rules of procedure are called for and their foundations are evident here.

An appendix to laws involving capital offences
21. 10–23

The series of rules which now follow in vv. 10–23 may best be regarded as an appendix to what has immediately preceded. The first three are concerned with matters of marriage and inheritance and appear to have been introduced at this point in the wake of the rules concerning warfare and women prisoners-of-war (20. 14). The final ruling in vv. 22–23 concerning the execution of a criminal follows up the rules regarding the need to avoid allowing a corpse to pollute the land.

The possibility that a woman prisoner-of-war might be taken as a wife (vv. 10–11) is fully accepted, and the fact that this appears to run counter to the general rule that the previous, non-Israelite inhabitants of the land were to be put to death is ignored. The ruling is undoubtedly ancient in origin and reflects what may often have occurred. In such a case the woman was to be allowed to mourn her lost parents, and no mention is made of the possibility that she may already have been married. The important point is made (vv. 12–13) that, once she had been taken as a wife she was to be granted the full status of such, on a level with that accorded to a native born Israelite, and her children were to be treated as full members of the family. Overall the family is regarded as a single integrated entity, with only the firstborn son's primogeniture conferring on him a unique status.

The verb used for 'let her go free' (v. 14) is also used of divorce (22. 19, 29) which is what is implied here. Having become a married woman, she was not to be sold as a slave. Any children are presumed to remain with the father. Even though the position of a divorced wife was weak and vulnerable, there is present nevertheless a desire to establish a basic minimum of 'citizen's rights' commensurate with Deuteronomy's claims that Israel was a nation of 'brothers and sisters'.

The case of a rejected wife leads on (vv. 15–17) to the broader issue of rights of inheritance and the special status of the firstborn son. The stories of Jacob and Esau (Gen. 48. 13–20; 49. 3–4) hinge on the possibility that the status of 'firstborn' son could be conferred by the father. The ancient Near-Eastern law codes of Ugarit and Nuzi reflect such flexibility and the question of royal succession in the Davidic court also indicates that the right of succession did not automatically fall to the eldest son. The status of children was one of the most persistent problems raised by polygamy. The ruling sets limits to the power of the father to intervene and make his will prevail over what was fair and just. The situation within a royal household, where there were customarily many wives, is most revealing and was especially complex. However, it may well not have conformed to normal practice. The act of acknowledgement referred to in v. 17 established a formal and legally binding situation. As the NRSV margin indicates the 'double portion' is literally 'two-thirds'. The privilege was necessary to ensure that the main bulk of the household estate remained a viable economic unit, rather than being parcelled out between several heirs.

The case of the rebellious son (vv. 18–21) links directly to the concern with the law regarding inheritance that has preceded it. Such a problem child could potentially ruin the entire household when the father died. Rather than risk this occurring, with disastrous consequences for all, such a son could, subject to certain safeguards, be put to death. The penalty is extreme and was undoubtedly meant as a deterrent. It was important that the accusation of the son's rebellious behaviour was not left as a responsibility for the parents alone (v. 19), but was to be investigated by the town elders. Only if they agreed could such a harsh sentence be carried out. Abuse of such a right by an irascible or unprincipled father had to be precluded. As with the preceding law, the concern is to establish limits, based on justice and openness to public accountability, to the authority of a father within his own family. The forms of ill-discipline mentioned seem relatively minor (v. 20), but are in agreement with the repeated concern for strict parental control which is to be found in the instructions of the Wisdom tradition. The aim was to avoid the ruination of the household, which was dependent on the hard work and commitment of each of its members. Profligate behaviour threatened everyone's livelihood! Finally, the participation of all the men of the town in an act of public stoning to death (v. 21) was a way of ensuring that responsibility for such a killing was acknowledged and shared by the community as a whole.

In the final law of the chapter the hanging up of the corpse of a person who had been executed (vv. 22–23) does not indicate that the execution took place by hanging. Rather the situation envisaged is that the executed person's corpse was put on public display as a deterrent in accordance with the principle of 19. 20. It was, however, not to be left exposed beyond the period of the day of execution. We see underlying the laws involving capital punishment a strong awareness of the solemn irrevocability of the taking of human life. Just as unatoned killing would pollute the land, so also even the corpse of a justly executed murderer required proper burial. The conflict of principle between the value of a deterrent display as a public warning and the need to avoid polluting the land was to be resolved by setting limits to the former action.

Boundaries of the community
22. 1–26. 19

The divine order of life
22. 1–12

The series of rulings which now follow cover a wide range of subject areas, but they have in common the need to maintain careful boundaries in order to uphold the divine order of life. If the preceding laws have focused primarily on the boundary between life and death, then these build on the recognition that hidden boundaries exist throughout the practical activities of daily life which must be observed and respected. The most self-evident examples concern the prohibitions on sowing another kind of seed between the rows of a vineyard (22. 5) and on making garments from two kinds of cloth (22. 11). Less obvious instances of a hidden boundary are reflected in the other rulings.

The insistence that an animal that has strayed onto another's property must be returned to its rightful owner (vv. 1–3) reflects deeply on the basis of ownership and property rights. Ownership of land was a fundamental feature of the social and economic structure of Israelite life. It provided the most basic form of 'goods' that an individual household might possess. Yet it was not an absolute right, which brought with it the claim that all that was found on it belonged to the landowner. Another's beasts might stray on it, or other objects might be left there. These still belonged to their original owners and

99

had to be returned to them, or kept until they reclaimed them (v. 2). The ruling affirms the priority of a right to private ownership over territorial rights, and gives fuller content to the prohibition on coveting another's property (cf. 5. 21).

Following this, the insistence on demanding action to assist an injured, or exhausted, animal (v. 4) appears at first to be an expression of compassion. Yet this is unlikely to have been the primary consideration which rests more on the prohibition *do not ignore it* (REB). Just as the fact that an animal had strayed was no excuse for misappropriating it (v. 1), so, in similar vein, the fact that a distressed animal did not belong to the person who saw it, was not a reason for failing to assist, and thereby preserve, it. Certain fundamental obligations crossed the hidden boundaries established by ownership.

A similar concern with the need to observe, and uphold, the hidden boundaries which exist in society motivates the prohibition directed against transvestism (v. 5). Although no punishment for infringement is set out, the declaration that such actions were 'abhorrent to the Lord your God' declares a strong level of repudiation. At the same time it recognizes that the practice might be difficult to take action against. Whether transvestism was thought to serve any religious purpose is unclear, but is not necessary towards explaining the ruling. The underlying assumption is that the distinction between the sexes is one of the foremost boundaries in life which must be maintained in respect of clothing.

A recognition that life must be allowed to prevail over death, thereby preserving the boundary between life and death, lies behind the ruling of vv. 6–7 protecting a bird's nest from being completely destroyed. It displays a degree of being 'environmentally friendly' in its fundamental concern to protect every species of birdlife. By acting with restraint so as to promote the continuance of the species, the Israelite would ensure that life prevails throughout the land. What might appear at first to be a minor matter is regarded as reaching into a more far-reaching principle concerning the promotion of life over death.

Once again in v. 8 actions are brought together that at first appear to be far removed from questions of bloodguilt, with all its ritual associations. The flat roof of a house was widely used for storage and for sleeping during the hotter months (cf. Jos. 2. 6; Judg. 16. 27). Without a protective parapet accidents could easily occur, so that the responsibility for avoiding them is placed on the builder of the house. Where a known risk was present, the negligent builder was held to be

100

responsible. In this case a subtle boundary is drawn to indicate where responsibility lies. The ruling bears interesting comparison with the allocation of responsibility for death caused by an ox (cf. Exod. 21. 28–32).

The need to observe the variety of species in their natural form, seen as a need to respect the created 'order' of the world is also to be seen in the ruling of 22. 9, although a slight uncertainty exists as to how tightly the ruling was applied. REB translates: *You are not to sow two kinds of seed between your vine rows* . . . which accords with the similar ruling in Lev. 19. 19 prohibiting the sowing of two kinds of seed in any one field more generally. The NRSV more narrowly understands the mixing of another crop with that of the vines to be a sufficient infringement of the prohibition on mixing two crops in one place. The background must generally be sought in the awareness that the creation of distinct species of animal and plant life was the result of an act of divine creation (cf. Gen. 1. 11–12). The distinctions of species were therefore to be respected and cross-fertilization between crops avoided. In this way the given divine order would be maintained and not wilfully crossed. Behind such concern we sense an anxiety to ensure that, in maintaining God's order, the life-giving quality of the soil would be protected to its fullest extent.

The prohibition against yoking together an ox and an ass (v. 10) is less motivated by a concern to place an unfair burden on the weaker animal, than a concern to avoid confusion in the given order of life. A desire to avoid miscegenation through sexual contact between species is also likely to have played a part.

Neither of the rulings concerning clothing in vv. 11–12 have yielded to any straightforward explanation. In the case of the prohibition on mixing two materials in making a garment (v. 11) it is the general concern to avoid confusing a natural distinction that is uppermost. The following ruling concerning the decoration of a garment (v. 12) has no obvious practical purpose. A parallel ruling of later origin in Num. 15. 37–41 explains the tassels as a reminder to Israelites of their obligations to God.

Sexual relationships
22. 13–30

The remaining section comprising 22. 13–30 is concerned with sexual relationships and is built up on the premiss that, after the life–death distinction, sexual differentiation was perceived as one of the most

101

basic of society's boundaries. Once this boundary had been crossed through sexual intercourse then a fundamental change in human relationships had occurred which demanded permanent recognition. Accordingly questions of virginity, marriage and rape called for special provisions.

The question of proof of virginity occupies the legislation in vv. 14–21. It is assumed that the husband will have paid a bride-price to the woman's family and that this will be on the understanding that she is a virgin. The 'evidence of virginity' is usually taken to be the bloodstains occurring after initial intercourse in marriage, but it may also be menstrual bloodstains from before marriage, serving as proof that the woman was not pregnant at that time. This would better accord with such evidence being available to the bride's parents, proving that they had not cheated the husband's family.

Verses 20–21 appear as a supplement to the major law. They are noteworthy in shifting responsibility for the woman's virginity from the parents to the woman herself. The law is extremely severe and, as in the case of a number of similar laws carrying the death penalty, the formula regarding the 'purging of evil' points to the intention of providing a deterrent. Throughout the legislation concerning virginity the primary concern clearly rested on the right of the husband to be able to claim the paternity of children born within his household. Any misconduct which jeopardized this expectation was threatened with the most dire consequences. The titillating narrative of promiscuity in Prov. 7. 6–23 indicates that reality did not always conform to the law. This is relevant later in showing that the situation confronted by Jesus in John 7. 53–8. 11 (NRSV; REB, because of the complex textual evidence, places the incident at the end of the Gospel after chapter 21) was not uncommon and that, although the Deuteronomic law was known, the severity of its penalty was regarded with anxiety (cf. also Matt. 5. 27–30). Consequently its application was often half-hearted and restrained!

The situation of a young woman *pledged in marriage* (vv. 23–27 NRSV 'engaged to be married') who is found in a sexual encounter with someone other than her betrothed raised the possibility that she was not a willing partner. This needed to be kept in mind in determining punishment for such conduct. In principle her status is presented as little different from that of a married woman, since her commitment would have entailed the completion of legal and financial obligations by both families. But she may have been the victim of rape and unable to defend herself (v. 27). The penalty determined therefore was that, in such cases, only the man was to be put to death. This is the point of drawing attention to the similarity with cases of murder (v. 26). An independent witness would be necessary for legal action to be taken, but is presumed to be unavailable.

In the case of a young woman who was not engaged, then compensation was payable to her father, and the culprit is compelled to take the woman as his wife. It is assumed that the father has been wronged because he would have lost the opportunity of obtaining a good bride price for her (v. 29). The ruling needs to be compared with the earlier one in Exod. 22. 16–17, which differs from Deuteronomy's in allowing that the father might not wish to give his daughter to the man. It is stipulated there that he is free to act accordingly, whereas the Deuteronomic ruling adds a prohibition on any possibility of a subsequent divorce. In both rulings the setting of compensation at fifty shekels should be regarded as a likely average amount for a bride price. In seducing the woman the man had crossed a sexual boundary and its consequences had to be dealt with as fairly as possible on the recognition that the extent to which the woman was a willing partner in what took place could not be proven.

The prohibition on marriage to a father's wife in v. 30 presumes that she would be a widowed step-mother. By making such a relationship the man would be crossing a boundary within the kin-group which had to be precluded.

Throughout these apparently miscellaneous rulings in which sexual behaviour is strongly to the fore the modern reader is struck by two features. The first is that the punishments appear draconian and that this has given rise to difficulties since it was essential that the same safeguards against innocent victims being wrongly punished needed to be taken into the reckoning as applied in cases of violent death. Secondly, the modern reader is surprised that these cases are made subject to prescribed punishments, and are not left to the wronged families to sort out privately. Yet the biblical legislation recognizes that these were issues in which society more generally was deeply concerned. In illicit sexual conduct hidden boundaries had been crossed and their existence required to be firmly reinstated. The 'social world' was seen to be a part of the 'natural world'. Consequently discerning the rules of this 'natural order' was important and these had to be upheld. The resort to severe punishments was evidently meant to have a deterrent effect since the problems of securing adequate evidence in some cases was recognized.

103

Membership of the community
23. 1–14

The laws of Deuteronomy have been compared very helpfully to the medieval concept of 'Privilege Law' in which the lord of a region was regarded as bound in a form of contract with the peasant-serfs who made up the region's population. In return for protecting these workers and providing them with the means of livelihood they were bound in obligations and duties to him, as lord. Similarly Deuteronomy regards the God of Israel as ' Lord and Master' and the people of Israel are God's servants, under obligation to observe the divine law.

A second feature of Deuteronomy is vitally significant. Ancient society had its primary roots in the extended family, identified in the Old Testament as 'fathers' houses' and 'tribes'. Authority and protection for individual households was channelled through this kinship structure. So, if a 'resident alien' was unable, or unwilling, to link up with a family, he or she became effectively marginalized. The 'foreigner' stood altogether outside this family group, but was generally assumed to have some protection from exploitation on account of his function (caravan traders and the like) or his accredited status (e.g. as a foreign emissary). In Deuteronomy the break-up of this older kinship-based social structure is shown to be well advanced. It is in process of being replaced with a new emphasis upon Israel as a single 'nation', upon the entire nation as a community of 'brothers and sisters', and upon the covenant relationship between Israel and the LORD God as the basis of this national existence. It comes as no surprise therefore that defining the boundaries of this community of God's people was an important goal of Deuteronomy's laws. In it ancient scruples concerning human individuality are interwoven with traditional and contemporary fears and enmities.

Sexuality was perceived to be a central feature of what it means to be 'human', enjoying the life-giving and life-affirming power of procreation. Accordingly, for a person to be sexually dismembered (v. 1), or to have been born as the result of an *irregular union* (v. 2) was regarded as a barrier from access to God. It is not altogether clear what was implied by such an irregular union (NIV 'forbidden marriage'), but we should think of prostitution, adulterous relationships and marriages outside the permitted degrees of affinity. Such sexual irregularity placed a person outside the tightly drawn sexual boundaries of the community so that the 'tenth generation' may simply be a way of denoting an unforeseeably long time; i.e. 'for ever'.

Prisoners were frequently dismembered to de-humanize them, and eunuchs appear to have been widely employed in ancient courts since having no immediate family dependants isolated them from dangerous family intrigues. The question of a eunuch's separation from God appears again in a prominent fashion in Isa. 56. 3–5; Acts 8. 27–39. In these instances there is a more generous and inclusive spirit.

The Ammonites and Moabites (v. 3) were settled in the region of the lower Jordan valley forming bitter rivals to Judah and Israel's southern tribes. Their exclusion from membership of Israel appears to have been based on long-held distrust and enmity. Gen. 19. 30–38 traces the origin of both peoples to a disreputable incestuous relationship between Lot and his daughters. The further historical reasons have been added later on the basis of biblical tradition.

According to Deut. 2. 29, the Moabites (v. 4) had sold food and water to the Israelites on their journey in the wilderness whereas no mention is made of the Ammonites acting likewise. The story of Ruth hinges in no small measure on awareness of this longstanding enmity between Israel and Moab. Balaam was a Moabite prophet whose misjudged attempts to prophesy against Israel are recounted in Num. 22. 1–24. 25.

The Edomites and Egyptians are treated more generously (vv. 7–8) in allowing migrants from these lands to become full members of the community in the third generation. Such action reflects the close ties, for trade and military protection, which emerged between these nations and Israel. The transition in the following section (vv. 9–14) to deal with matters of hygiene points to an awareness that different patterns and practices in this regard motivated a feeling that certain foreign migrants could not be absorbed into the 'holy' nature of the Israelite community.

The need to ensure rigid hygiene in military encampments was clearly based on long-term experience of the dangerous conditions that frequently prevailed in such camps. The long campaigns, prolonged periods of siege warfare, and the racial intermixture of the soldiery all contributed to making military operations disease-ridden and unhealthy for both combatants and non-combatants alike. We should compare Isa. 10. 16 for threats of 'wasting disease' breaking out among besieging troops and the visitation of the 'angel of the LORD' of Isa. 37. 36 has frequently been understood as a theological cover title for disease.

That nocturnal sexual emissions marked a loss of the holy 'life force', and could be the consequence of disease called for care in this regard (cf. Lev. 16–17). In similar vein the the need for toilet ablutions, especially in military encampments, reflects belief in the direct presence of God marching with Israel into battle. This belief is well focused in the ancient hymn to the God of the Ark (Num. 10. 33–34) and is still retained in the picture of God advancing at the head of his people in their return to their homeland (Isa. 40. 9; 49. 10; 52. 12). Belief in God's leadership to give victory in battle colours the Deuteronomic understanding of warfare as a 'holy' enterprise. This necessitated that scruples concerning holiness were not to be carelessly overridden in time of war.

The marking out of a 'designated area' (NRSV) as a latrine is literally a 'hand'; accordingly REB renders it as *a sign*. There appears a degree of awareness that disease could be spread through human excrement so the concern was to prevent the uncontrolled spread of anything unclean. The *trowel* of v. 13 (NIV has 'something to dig with'), uses a word which elsewhere denotes a stake, or tent-peg.

Protecting the community
23. 15–25

The right of a slave to claim protection and to live as a free citizen without fear of being returned to a former master (v. 15) marks an unexpected concession, related to Deuteronomy's larger concern with protecting the more marginalized members of the community. They are judged to deserve the same protection as would be granted to any full member. It marks an extension of the law of Exod. 22. 21 which forbade oppression of an alien. Such protection runs counter to the customary rule in the ancient Near East where, significantly, the Code of Hammurabi demanded the death penalty for harbouring runaway slaves. It marks a step in Deuteronomy's striving towards a concept of 'human rights'. The issue is further reflected in the New Testament in St Paul's Epistle to Philemon, where the apostle, in sending back the runaway slave Onesimus to his former master, commends his acceptance as a 'brother in Christ'.

Temple prostitution (v. 18) of both sexes appears to have been quite widely practised in antiquity (cf. Gen. 38. 21–22; I Kgs. 14. 24; Hos. 4. 14). The firm prohibition in Israel (v. 17) enforced here suggests that such prostitutes as were to be found were usually of foreign origin. Mic. 1. 7 refers to prostitutes' fees being regularly paid into the temple treasury. The term for *male prostitute* is literally a 'dog'; the noun is used in both a sharply negative and pejorative sense, as here, but also in a more positive manner to indicate a faithful follower.

The law of 23. 19–20 concerning the prohibition of taking interest from a fellow Israelite revises the earlier ruling of Exod. 22. 25–27. The extension to cover goods and property generally is a new development. The problems of transition to a moneyed economy, the rules of surety and the prohibition of taking interest reflect the difficulties in ancient Israel of maintaining effective control of finance and preventing exploitation through excessive demands (usury). Poor harvests and periodic droughts rendered occasional loans to a needy neighbour imperative (cf. 15. 7–11), whereas loans for commercial enterprise served a different purpose and were treated with greater distrust (cf. Eccles. 5. 13–15).

The rule that a vow, once made, must be adhered to (vv. 21–23) is further reflected on in Eccles. 5. 4–5; cf. also Mark 7. 9–13. for the use of vows to avoid other obligations. Vows formed an important feature of religious activity, covering voluntary gifts and sacrifices, especially in thanksgiving for recovery from sickness and similar experiences of divine help.

The two laws concerning the freedom to eat from a neighbour's vineyard or field of grain (vv. 24–25) reflect what was evidently an ancient concession made to travellers. The privilege was not, however, to be abused by seeking to make a profit from it.

From the modern preacher's perspective the great variety of rulings in this chapter may appear remote and strange. They are, however, all concerned with defining the boundaries of the ancient Israelite community and they take account of the complex nature of the factors which determine this. Even a brief reflection highlights how relevant many of those concerns have remained in modern society, and how prevalent are their attendant problems. The preoccupation with individual rights and the fulfilment of private and personal goals which dominate modern Western life-styles encourage all too easily a disregard of the larger social dimension. Those citizens who become marginalized through economic, ethnic or sexual considerations find modern society a difficult environment in which to survive. Their existence highlights the fact that societies build up hidden boundaries through a natural process of growth which are established and marked by many factors. These boundaries are often hard to define, and sometimes even to identify, and they are frequently harder still to justify. They impinge nevertheless very strongly on the quality of life for individuals. To reflect on what ancient Israel defined as the boundaries of its own social world, imposes a requirement for the modern reader to do likewise and to seek a better understanding of the problems and dangers presented by our present-day 'hidden boundaries'.

Laws of compassion and care
24. 1–25. 3

After a series of laws which define the scope of Israel as a divine community we now have a short collection which is aimed at establishing its nature and the quality of life it should embrace. The first two such rulings return to the subject of marriage, but fit into this new section because they serve to uphold the dignity and status accorded to marriage within Israel.

The ruling of vv. 1–4 that a woman, once divorced and remarried, cannot thereafter return to her former husband is unique to Deuteronomy. Even though it allows divorce simply on the decision of the husband (vv. 1 and 3), its importance lies in its broader aim to protect the institution of marriage. What is implied in v. 1 by *something offensive in her* (NRSV 'something objectionable') is not clear. The law is however, informative in setting out the procedure for divorce. The husband must present a written document to the woman, give it to her personally, and then send her out of the house. The formula that a return to her former husband would be 'abominable to the LORD' suggests that such a remarriage was rejected because it represented a confusion within the community. The woman's becoming 'unclean' cannot be because she had remarried, which was in any case to be expected, but because her return to her first husband would reduce his former rejection to an act of irresponsible frivolity. The law rules out casual 'wife-swapping'. In a larger biblical context the ruling has proved significant in its relevance to understanding Hos. 3 and the relationship between the prophet Hosea and Gomer. The marriage of two people is seen as a status in which the community as a whole has an interest so that it cannot be reduced to the level of a private arrangement between two, or three, individuals.

The law regarding exemption from military service for one year after marriage (24. 5) is in line with the rules governing liability for such duty set out in 20. 5–7. Its aim was to protect the community as far as was practicable from the risks and threats posed by war. It sought to enable the newly established household to produce a child, hopefully a male heir, and so provide a basis for the renewal of the community after the conflict. Also, if the husband were killed, it would reduce the risk that the widow would be left childless (cf. Ruth 1. 12).

The bottom line of poverty comes starkly to the fore in the ruling of v. 6 which prohibited the taking of even one millstone in pledge to secure a debt. This regarded the possession of millstones as the most essential utensils for a self-supporting household. Without the means to grind flour the last vestige of independence would be lost. The ruling is one of a number of laws which sharply focuses Deuteronomy's concern to prevent the application of unrestrained economic rights from undermining the compassion of the community. Law had a responsibility for protecting commerce but it also needed to make sure that such rigidity did not undermine the basic human compassion commensurate with living as the people of God.

The prohibition of kidnapping (v. 7) follows the earlier law of Exod. 21. 16. Such a crime was evidently a widely practised consequence of banditry, undertaken in order to sell the victims as slaves. These appear often to have been children and the prophetic condemnation of *selling honest folk for silver* (Amos 2. 6) may have applied both to such criminal activity, as well as to debt-slavery. All such exploitation of one human being by another constituted an affront to the ideal of 'a nation of brothers and sisters'. It represents a serious limitation here that the prohibition is applied only to a fellow Israelite.

The *virulent skin disease* of v. 8 is not identified more closely, but cannot have been the 'leprosy' of earlier English versions, since this was not known in the Near East in biblical times. NEB translates as 'malignant skin disease', but this implies skin cancer, and is also unlikely. The noun used to describe the affliction is also used of buildings, indicating that its nature was not precisely identified, but was indicative of any condition that was thought to be potentially infectious. Deuteronomy consistently reveals a strong concern with all forms of disease, pointing to the role of the levitical priests in making a diagnosis and prescribing medication. The mention of Moses' sister Miriam in v. 9 recalls the incident of Num. 12. 14–15 when she was temporarily stricken with a skin disease as a divine punishment for rebelling against Moses.

The concern to establish a basic minimum of citizen's 'rights' is well illustrated in the ruling of 24. 10 –13 which regards every free citizen's home as a private domain – the owner's 'castle'. It was not to be entered without a specific invitation. At the same time the bottom edge of poverty is illustrated by the refusal to permit a cloak, pledged as security for a loan, to be retained overnight. Home and basic clothing formed a necessary part of living a fully human existence. Both this, and the following ruling of vv. 14–15 that a worker's wages were to be paid promptly on the day they were earned, show how the gap between the rich and the poor could easily deprive the latter of access to normal public justice and respect. The law endeavours to counter this. Wages would be differently valued according to the measure of human need. So any failure to pay them promptly could lead to undeserved destitution. The warning that failure to comply would incur God's anger shows a recognition, in regard to this ruling as well as the two that precede it, that no effective punishment could be readily imposed for such bad conduct.

The ruling of v. 16 that parents were not to be punished for offences committed by their children and vice versa sets an important limit to the implementation of the age-old convention of blood revenge in family feuds. It establishes an important principle of human individuality. Elsewhere in the Old Testament stories are to be found where entire households are punished on the assumption that a collective guilt pervades it (cf. Jos. 7. 24–26; cf. also Num. 16. 27, 31–32). It is noteworthy that these 'household' punishments involved offences against the rules of holiness. Against this taboo-laden assumption that these sins incurred a kind of infection, the emerging legal tradition displays a growing sensitivity to individual responsibility. In this regard it marks a major moral advance. The issue became a major one in coming to terms with experiences of national failure so as to leave room for individual repentance and an acceptance of personal commitment (cf. Jer. 31. 31; Ezek. 18. 1–32).

That the rise of Israel's national legal tradition sought to bring greater protection and help for those who were the most marginalized members of the community is to be seen in the rulings of vv. 17–21. By insisting that resident aliens and orphans were not to be cheated of justice, and that a widow was not to be deprived of her cloak under any circumstances, the law sought to establish a minimal basis of human rights. Even though the actual examples cited may appear to be relatively minor and elementary, it is a matter of primary interest that Israel's emerging legal tradition was used to restructure the shape of society and to use its authority to aim towards a basic quality of life for even the poorest.

A comparable concern to give the force of legal authority to what would otherwise have remained only the haphazard conventions of public charity is to be found in the rulings which give the force of law to the right that gleanings from the harvest must be left for the poorer members of society to gather (vv. 19–22).

It is important to note that the call to remember the origins of Israel in the slavery of Egypt (v. 18) is used to provide a motive for the acceptance of rulings which those who formulated them were well aware could all too easily be ignored. Those who believed that charity was a good idea, but should be a matter of individual choice, were forced to face up to a larger awareness that it formed an obligation upon every member of the community. In its essential demand it was based on the principle of 'a nation of brothers and sisters' under God's covenant. Many of the laws lack effective penalties which could be imposed on those who failed to heed their injunctions. They nevertheless recognized that compassion and justice needed to go hand in hand.

The circumstances in which a dispute between two persons might lead to the imposition of a punishment of flogging on the party judged to be guilty (25. 1–3) are left wholly unclear. The ruling indicates that such punishments were available to a judge to determine but required that he, or another judge, be present when the punishment was carried out. The stipulation of a maximum of forty lashes is a further example of the aim of using the law to monitor legal procedures and punishments thereby undergirding them with some measure of religious compassion. Even a convicted offender was not to be deprived of basic human rights. That the number of lashes was to be related to 'the gravity of the offence' accords with the retributive concept of justice. Later Judaism restricted the punishment to thirty-nine lashes, so that no accidental infringement could occur; cf. II Cor. 11. 24.

Protecting the family
25. 4–19

The ruling concerning not muzzling a working ox (25. 4) comes strangely in its present location, although the general concern for the welfare of domestic animals accords with other laws. Its inclusion at this point raises questions whether it was meant to be taken literally. In I Cor. 9. 9 it is understood by Paul as illustrative of the broader principle that a worker is worthy of his wages. Here, however, it is followed by laws dealing with sexual matters, strongly hinting that there is a hidden sexual reference, or at least a deliberate measure of

111

ambiguity, with the ox symbolizing sexual potency. The laws that follow are aimed at protecting a man's expectations of producing offspring, if necessary by a brother's intervention.

The most striking of the rulings is that of vv. 5–10, concerning the so-called levirate marriage (from the Hebrew *levir* = 'husband's brother'). The ruling was aimed at keeping the dead man's estate intact in the event of his death. It appears to be based on the assumption that another brother remained living in the household and points to a situation when both brothers, with their father probably still living, formed part of one extended family. The ruling is focused on preservation of the brother's name and the preservation of his estate. Overall the concern appears to be the prevention of the break-up of the household into weak and uneconomic units, as a result of misfortune. However there are also strong undercurrents of honour and reputation involved, as the concern with maintaining the dead brother's name (v. 6) shows.

The eventual birth of a son and his bearing the name of the deceased would certainly appear to imply a limitation to the status of the new husband and father. It is this requirement which is recognized as likely to cause the greatest difficulty, rather than the making provision for a widow. The humiliation specified in vv. 9–10 for a refusal to take responsibility for the widow and to build up the brother's house points to such a perspective. However, many aspects of the ruling remain obscure, and must have been subject to individual circumstances. It appears directed at affirming a principle, comparable to that which gave a major share of the family estate to the firstborn (21. 15–17) and there is an unexpressed assumption that the deceased person's family would naturally seek to preserve his name.

The likelihood that the surviving brother would be unwilling to fulfil the obligation (vv. 7–10) is frankly recognized, apparently because to do so would mean sacrificing his own future status and prospects in the interests of protecting those of his deceased brother. Quite evidently the obligations of brotherhood could be far-reaching and readily led to rivalry where half-brothers were concerned. It should not be ruled out of reckoning that a significant reason for recording the law may have been to limit the penalties which could be enforced on the surviving brother if he chose to opt out of the levirate requirement. It is assumed that the family of the deceased would expect to see his name and position upheld, and might have resorted to harsh measures in an attempt to enforce this. If so, the ruling carries a larger significance in marking another instance of legislation (cf. 21.

18–21) which limited the authority of the head of an extended family group over its members.

The removal of the sandal (v. 9) may convey some element of sexual imagery in the refusal to accept marital obligations, or be a piece of legal symbolism exemplifying the refusal to accept ownership of (i.e. walk on) a brother's property. Overall the retention of the law leaves several aspects of its operation in doubt, although its background in recognizing the need to protect a family estate in the event of misfortune striking one of its leading figures is evident.

The text of the ruling of vv. 11–12 indicates that, in the event of a brawl between men, a woman is to be severely punished if she takes hold of the genitals of her husband's opponent. The inference is that she is likely to have deliberately injured him in the process or had sought to do so. This is the only Old Testament law which prescribes mutilation as a punishment, although the sense of the 'law of retribution' in 19. 21 implies its general application. Behind it lies the unexpressed anxiety that any action which could damage a man's prospects of fatherhood constituted a major offence. Accordingly the punishment was severe and a link with the preceding law established.

A new area of crime is brought under review in vv. 13–16 with the fraudulent use of weights and measures in commerce. Such cheating was evidently a persistent problem (cf. Ps. 12. 2; Prov. 20. 10, 23; Amos 8. 5) and the attempts to counter it are exemplified in the establishing of offical (royal) standards for measurement. Even so, the inevitable wear of stone, or metal, weights as well as regional variations and the ease with which such cheating could be perpetrated necessitated periodic reappraisals and reforms. The formula that those who cheat in this way are *abominable to the* LORD (v. 16) indicates that shame and opprobrium were seen to offer the chief means of countering such dishonesty.

The reference in vv. 17–19 to the Amalekites is to the narrative of Exod. 17. 8–17. The intensity of Israel's hatred of this people is reflected in the account of Saul's defeat of them leading to the controversial slaughter of the Amalekite king Agag (I Sam. 15. 1–33). The Deuteronomic author has introduced the details of the manner in which the Amalekites attacked Israel, apparently out of desire to explain the intensity of Israel's hostility towards them. The reason for including this reminder (v. 18) of the need for maintaining such a deeply felt ethnic hatred is unclear but may be to suggest an alignment of the unrelenting hatred of certain peoples with particular forms of criminal conduct.

113

12. 1–26. 19   *The Deuteronomic Law Code*

The collection of laws which make up the Deuteronomic code is here brought to an end, since what follows are two liturgical confessions which reaffirm the religious context in which the laws are given. When seen as a whole the laws offer a necessary filling-out of what it means to observe and keep the commandments of God. On one hand they support the institution of laws and legal officials as a welcome means of upholding Israel's obedience to God's covenant. At the same time they recognize that living as a community of God's covenant people demands more than simply being 'law-abiding' in a narrow sense. It calls for a right attitude towards all fellow-citizens, a perpetual recollection of Israel's vulnerable and disadvantaged origins, a willingness to empathize with the most marginal elements of the community and a goal of creating prosperity as a privilege to be shared, not selfishly indulged.

Receiving and remembering
26. 1–11

Chapter 12 introduced the code of laws with detailed instructions concerning the central sanctuary where prayers were to be offered and to which sacrificial offerings were to be brought. Now at its conclusion two confessional recitals are prescribed, the first in vv. 5–10 to accompany the offering of firstfruits and the second in vv. 13–15 to accompany the giving of the third-year tithe. These confessions give content and direction to the demand for worship and provide an oblique affirmation of the nature and character of Israel's God. They thereby encase the laws within a framework of religious understanding in much the same way that the laws themselves are modified and infused with a host of religious features calling for compassion and commitment to the welfare of the entire nation.

The confession prescribed to accompany the offering of firstfruits has been extensively discussed since it comes as close as any short passage can to expressing Israel's 'creed'. It also provides an outline summary of the central 'plot' of Israel's story from Genesis to Joshua. To what extent this outline story of Israel's origins was itself a construction of the Deuteronomists, or was of much earlier origin, has been variously understood. Certainly Deuteronomy has given to it a distinctive vocabulary and has woven into each of its main episodes a unique valuation (e.g. the wilderness wanderings as a time of testing). The summary that is set out here therefore is a highly significant feature of the nature of Israel's faith through its portrayal of particular

114

historical episodes of the nation's past as a reflection of the nature of the relationship between Israel and God. In large measure it explains Israel's unique identity as a people in terms of this continuing relationship. The set wording of the confessions also ensured that each succeeding generation of Israelites saw themselves as drawn into this relationship and were able to focus their social attitudes and identify their obligations on the basis of it.

Because Deuteronomy is cast in the form of a speech by Moses before the people had crossed over the River Jordan to enter the land, the forward look of v. 1 is necessary. Throughout Deuteronomy the historical past, the narrative 'present' of the time of Israel's point of entry into the land, and the 'real' present of the reader are all subtly woven into one experience, calling for an appropriate response to God. The offering of firstfruits for the support of the levitical priests is required by Deut. 18. 3–5. Here in v. 2 the offering is to provide the material of the feast for rejoicing before the LORD God in which the priests and other marginalized citizens are to share (v. 11).

The Deuteronomic understanding of time as charged with religious significance by the fulfilment of a divine promise is well displayed in the confessional *I acknowledge this day* . . . (v. 3). God has been faithful; it is now up to Israel to respond accordingly. By giving the basket to the priest who is then required to set it down before the altar (v. 4) the action is identified as the worshipper's gift to God. The *homeless Aramaean* (NRSV 'wandering Aramaean') of v. 5 emphasizes the point that the ancestor possessed no land of his own. The reference would appear to be to Jacob-Israel, the ancestor of the nation, but the lack of a specific name may be intentional in showing that the entire nation was at one time without a land.

The point that Jacob's offspring grew into a nation by sheer increase of numbers is a distinctively Deuteronomic viewpoint. The concept of nationhood is variously understood in the Old Testament and Exod. 19. 6 recalls the making of the covenant on Mount Sinai (Horeb) as the moment at which Israel became constituted as 'a holy nation'. Deuteronomy is concerned with what it requires for Israel to be a nation, with a major focus on territory and a weakened attention to the bonds of kinship. Possession of land, constitutional government and family ties of kinship each contributed one part towards making Israel what it is. However, most important of all was the covenant with the LORD God which bound all these features together and defined Israel as a community of God. The point is historically significant, since the attention to nationhood, and the emphasis that a

115

divine promise lay at the back of this, gave rise to a flexibility of understanding. God's covenant undergirded the historical reality of being a nation and this conviction underpinned Israel's ability to survive the disasters of 587 BCE. Faith and commitment, rather than land and political independence, became the badges of a spiritual citzenship.

The oppressive nature of Egyptian rule over Israel's ancestors (v. 7) is in line with the portrayal in the exodus stories of the tyrannical and irrational actions of the Egyptian Pharaoh. Such portrayal, however, is not so much anti-Egyptian (cf. Deut. 23. 7–8; Isa. 19. 18–22) as anti-tyrannous. We have seen that 23. 7 allows a third-generation Egyptian to become a full member of the Israelite nation. The support afforded by miraculous divine actions in rescuing the nation's ancestors from slavery (v. 8) is a very important Deuteronomic emphasis. Unaided and without any means of self-defence, the Israelites would have been doomed to a life of slavery, but were instead rescued by God's mastery over the natural world (the plagues that struck Egypt) working through the leadership of Moses (against which the Israelites frequently rebelled). God was the Great Provider, no matter how weak, helpless and faltering were his worshippers.

A distinctive feature of the confession is the concern to identify the firstfruits as the product of the land which God had given to Israel (v. 10), and not simply as the result of the divine power to give fertility to the soil. Consistently Deuteronomy shows restraint in pointing to fertility as a mysterious divine potency working in the soil, preferring to draw attention to the wider historical and social dimensions in which the blessings of God were received. Consistently the dangers of the popular cults of Baal and Astarte as deities who gave 'life' (i.e. fertility) were recognized and repudiated on account of their undesirable sexual connections.

Do not forget those less fortunate
26. 12–19

According to 14. 22–26 an annual tithe was to be set aside and used to provide a feast for the family at the sanctuary appointed by God. The third-year tithe which is mentioned here was a separate special offering given for the support of the Levites, and is here more widely designated for the benefit of aliens, widows and orphans. The giving of this additional tithe is made into an affirmation of a total willingness to abide by the obligations of the divine covenant (v. 13). By disposing of the tithe in the required manner the giver declared an unreserved commitment to God. That no mention is made of the revelation of the law on Mount Horeb in the recital of Israel's origins in the confession of 26. 5–10 can only be because such a revelation and its demands were implicitly acknowledged by the act of bringing the firstfruits and tithes.

In what appears as an additional reminder the worshipper is called upon to keep fully in mind the traditional restrictions on what was implied by holiness (v. 14). These meant refraining from contact with uncleanness and death, and might have been overlooked. The presence of the clause at this point is significant since Deuteronomy gives a very strong impetus to the ethical and social interpretation of holiness as a basis of community compassion. At the same time older constraints, drawn from taboo-based cultic scruples, could not be ignored altogether and so they are reaffirmed here. Much of this inter-weaving of ethical and taboo-based (ritual) concerns in understand-ing holiness remained current in Jewish life for a considerable period.

The concluding appeal to God for blessing (v. 15) returns to a central aspect of Deuteronomy's theological understanding of worship and the interpretation of the sanctuary with all its ritual activities. Essentially it can be no more than a place where God may be approached and where the divine name may be invoked. It cannot be the place where God resides, as had traditionally been assumed in the language of psalmody, for this can only be in heaven – God's 'holy dwelling-place'.

A final commendation of the law code, and the central place that it is to occupy in Israel's life as a community in covenant with the LORD God is presented in vv. 16–19. Its renewed emphasis upon 'this day' (note especially the threefold repetition in vv. 16, 17 and 18) returns to the central Deuteronomic perspective of worship as a means whereby past, present and future generations are bound together in a shared experience of encounter with God. Each generation stands, or falls, where its ancestors stood or fell away, in their confrontation with God. The time for renewing obedience is always 'now'. The potentially universal nature of the affirmation that God will set Israel *high above all the nations which he has made* (v. 19) should not be over-looked. All nations are the creation of the one God, but Israel's position is understood as unique and special. What is implied by this exaltation of one nation over others is not further spelt out, but is tied to the concept of holiness.

117

Part III

Epilogue to the Law Book

27. 1–34. 12

The administration of the law
27. 1–30. 20

The conclusion of the law book within Deuteronomy is followed by an epilogue which gives instructions for the visible memorializing of it. This epilogue then spells out with illustrative detail the contrasting consequences of obedience and disobedience to it. Good or bad responses will lead to blessing or curse, with the latter predominating. Overall this imbalance leaves an impression that there is more that can go wrong than can go right, once the law has been received and acknowledged. This cannot, however, have been the intention, but is best seen as the outworking of two features which affect Deuteronomy as a whole. The first is the general sense of crisis, bordering on despair, which the reader is presumed to feel when surveying the catalogue of disasters and misfortunes which had overtaken the nation. Why had these happened? The answer is sought in pointing to Israel's disregard of God's law. A second influence may be found in the extent to which ancient Near-Eastern, predominantly Assyrian, treaty formulations have provided a pattern for the language and structure of Deuteronomy. These documents make extensive use of intimidatory curse-formulations as a means of putting pressure on the signatories of the treaty. They amount to a firm threat of punishment and woe for those who renege on their obligations. Deuteronomy has evidently developed this pattern further as a rhetorical device for placing the law in the forefront of the nation's consciousness. Woe betide those who do not heed its demands!

A memorial to the law
27. 1–10

The best-known of ancient Near-Eastern law codes outside of the Bible is that of the Babylonian ruler Hammurabi (or Hammurapi, c.1790–1750 BCE), which consists of a large inscribed stone tablet, set up as a boundary marker to make known to travellers that they were entering a land of justice and good order. Deuteronomy here envisages a similar role for the laws which have been given. The instructions for the recording of them on stone tablets erected on the west side of the Jordan enlarge upon the instructions for blessing and cursing on Mount Ebal and Mount Gerizim given earlier in 11. 29–30. It begins with an instruction to act immediately after crossing the Jordan (v. 2) which suggests a location close to Gilgal, situated on the banks of the River Jordan. Mount Ebal (v. 4) would be some distance further west. The time reference, however, may be taken to mean 'promptly', with the location on Mount Ebal in mind. The coating of plaster over the stone conformed to conventional practice to make the task of inscribing letters onto the surface much easier and to make them more legible.

The extent to which such inscribed public monuments imply a general level of public literacy is questionable (v. 3). Stone tables of laws served as symbols of territorial jurisdiction and were a form of royal propaganda. Yet, in their underlying formulation as official documents, they fulfilled a vital social role as guides for those involved in legal administration. It appears that rulings were usually based on case-records from actual proceedings drawn up by trained officials. Overarching this, the element of royal authority in the case of such a great figure as Hammurabi was vital, as the divine (Mosaic) authority was similarly vital to Israel's covenant law.

The instruction of v. 4 follows what has already been commanded in vv. 2–3, and links the law tablets with a further action to the earlier one focused on the building of an altar. However, these instructions, together with the arrangement for publicly declaring blessings and curses on Mount Gerizim and Mount Ebal respectively (11. 29–30), all appear to have been combined into a single concerted action aimed at memorializing Israel's entry into the land. At this point the Samaritan text of the Pentateuch identifies the location as the Samaritan holy mountain, Mount Gerizim, and it remains uncertain how and when the traditions of the location diverged. Deuteronomy is concerned to

119

focus attention on the centrality of law as the subject of this memorial since such laws were to shape, for good or ill, the lives of those who would live in the new land.

The building of the altar commanded in v. 5 occasions considerable surprise since it contravenes both the spirit and the letter of the strict instructions given in 12. 1–27 that only at the one central sanctuary (Jerusalem) were offerings to be made. Its inclusion frankly recognizes that, at one time, an altar had existed on Mount Ebal and further reflects the fact that Deuteronomy's strict rule regarding centralization of worship was a relatively late introduction into its national charter. The stones for the altar were to be kept in their natural state (v. 6), without dressing by human tools since this would be to alter their assumed God-given state. The precise meaning of the *shared offerings* (REB) referred to in v. 7 has been much discussed. NRSV reads 'sacrifices of well-being' and earlier versions translated the Hebrew as 'peace offerings'. The underlying sense appears to be that of 'making whole, complete', but whether this refers to the mending of broken relationships or making a person 'whole' is not determined.

In v. 8 the text returns to the issue of the text of the law and ties in the mention of the altar stones with those for the inscribing of the law, even though the two purposes are distinct. In general it appears that it is Deuteronomic concern with the law which has necessitated further elaboration of the instructions for an altar. The reference to an awesome silence (v. 9) brings out well the sense of the original covenant-making on Mount Horeb and the fact that it was now reaffirmed on the eve of entry into the land. The goal of thirty-eight years of wilderness wanderings was now reached and the crossing into the promised land would shortly be made.

Twelve curses
27. 11–26

The series of twelve curses set out in vv. 14–26, which the Levites are to declare publicly and to which a response of 'Amen' is made by the people, reflects a firmly stereotyped tradition, which was almost certainly ancient and independent of Deuteronomy. It has been incorporated here since it could be readily associated with the curse tradition of Mount Ebal. That there also once existed corresponding series of blessings, taking the form 'Blessed are . . .' and used as a teaching formula, as reflected in the New Testament Beatitudes, may be plausibly surmised. On the evidence of the particular forms of conduct that are condemned in these twelve curses we can recognize activities which were deeply undesirable and condemned, but which were likely to fall outside the effective scope of the law. They are broadly associated with conduct which is condemned in the laws as being *abominable to the* LORD *your God* (cf. 25. 16 with 27. 15).

Infringements of the second commandment by making an image of any kind, which forms the subject of the first curse (v. 15), have already been roundly condemned. The distinctive feature here is that such an image is set up 'in secret' and so was hidden from the eyes of the people generally. By making the affirmation 'Amen' the citizen declares his, or her, wholehearted participation in the cursing. How God would punish any offender is then left open.

The definition of the offender in the second curse of v. 16 as *anyone who slights his father or his mother* (REB) appears rather weak. NRSV reads 'who dishonours father or mother' (similarly NIV) and the close parallels in Exod. 21. 17; Lev. 20. 9 read 'curse'. The precise nature of such reprehensible conduct is left open and the fifth commandment recasts the wording into a positive form as 'Honour your father and your mother' (5. 16). Any form of verbal abuse of parents is what is repudiated.

The curse dealing with the problem of the illegal removal of boundary stones in v. 17 returns to an issue already covered in the law code in 19. 14. Its repetition here simply reflects the difficulty already noted that the offence was a complex one to deal with on account of the near-impossibility of establishing proof.

The misdirection of a blind person (v. 18), usually as a cruel form of joke, is prohibited in the law of Lev. 19. 14. Similarly the depriving of the most marginalized members of the community from obtaining justice (v. 19) is brought into the sphere of curse here, although it has already been made the subject of admonition (cf. 24. 17). The forms of sexual activity repudiated and placed under a curse in vv. 20–23 strongly suggest that they refer to acts of sexual abuse in a household, rather than to infringements of the limitations on marriage unions. The latter were already covered by legal provisions, but sexual abuse of women living in a household and carried out privately, without intention or prospect of marriage to the abuser, appears the most likely target of a curse of the kind detailed here.

The curse on sexual union with an animal (v. 21) may perhaps reflect the knowledge that such actions were permitted, and even encouraged, in some ancient religious traditions. In these the animal was regarded as a symbol of divine potency so that union with such a

121

beast was believed to confer power. The offence is similarly outlawed in Exod. 22. 19 (cf. also Lev. 20. 13–16). Marriage to a half-sister (v. 22) was permissible according to Gen. 20. 12; (cf. II Sam. 13. 13) but is prohibited in Lev. 18. 9; 20. 17, and marriage to a mother-in-law (v. 23) is prohibited in Lev. 18. 17; 20. 14.

The indication that the action of inflicting violent bodily harm on another person (v. 24) refers to a deed carried out 'in secret' provides the reason why it required a separate curse. Had it come to public knowledge then legal redress might have been available. The general and comprehensive nature of the final curse of v. 26 must certainly indicate that it has been included in order to bring the number of such curses up to twelve. This brought them into line with the theoretical number of Israel's tribes and was itself a suitably 'whole and complete' number.

The terms of God's covenant with Israel
28. 1–29. 1

The brief list of twelve curses which have just been listed clearly fulfilled a social role in the life of the community, serving as a joint affirmation of conduct that the Israelite community would not tolerate. They gave forcible expression to the affirmation that certain actions and types of behaviour were 'abominable to God' (and so to God's people!). The series that now unfolds extensively in chapter 28 clearly had a different origin and a different purpose altogether. It concludes in 29. 1 with a summarizing statement that the choice between the way of blessing and the way of curse constitutes the terms of the covenant made in the plains of Moab. The kernel of this chapter is certainly to be seen in vv. 3–6 and 16–19 which contain two sets of roughly parallel utterances, first of blessing and then of curse. The origin of these sayings must certainly be sought in a context of worship where they formed a part of the prayerful admonition of all that holiness implied.

However, this original kernel of blessings and curses has subsequently been greatly extended and amplified in a markedly literary fashion. Their purpose has now become didactic and reflective, rather than social and ethical. Moreover it is the list of curses that has received the greatest amplification. A significant literary point that has been widely accepted by scholars is that the Deuteronomic authors appear here to be familiar with, and to have adapted for their own use, the form of intimidatory curses that constituted a part of

122

Assyrian international treaty documents. What we find therefore are no longer properly curses at all, but rather threats concerning the penalties which will befall those who disobey the demands of God's law, in the same way that the Assyrian emperor threatened any of his vassals who disobeyed his will. Those who had signed up to the treaty (under compulsion) were warned of the consequences of any defection.

The curses in the list ascribed to Moses similarly far outweigh in number the promised blessings. A second noteworthy feature is that, in the later sections of the list, they allude quite specifically to events and disasters which had already, by the author's time, befallen Israel as a nation. Beginning with misfortunes of a general, and widely experienced, nature, the series becomes increasingly pointed so as to mirror events that took place in Judah and Jerusalem during the twilight days of the old kingdom. So their purpose is subtly altered in order to use the curse formula as a way of explaining these tragedies in terms of God's anger against a disobedient people. They compel the reader to ask the question 'How is God's love for Israel present in the light of these tragic events?' An answer to this question is sought in pointing to Israel's failure to keep God's law.

In the opening list of blessings and curses (vv. 1–14) the fact that agriculture and warfare are central reveals those areas of primary risk which shaped the quality of life in ancient Israel. A second section begins in v. 15 and extends as far as v. 46. It enumerates frustrations and misfortunes of daily living in terms of poverty, crop failure, disease and defeat in battle. The curse is that Israel would find that on every path of activity on which it embarked, failure would greet it. From v. 20 the terminology employed makes it clear that it is the LORD God who will be directly effecting the curses which will fall upon Israel.

Disease figures prominently among these misfortunes (v. 22) and it is a noteworthy feature of Deuteronomy that this is directly understood to be inflicted by God. Accordingly the listing of the various forms of sickness in this verse, and again in vv. 27–28, 35, is noteworthy in showing why modern scholars have experienced difficulty in making a clear diagnosis of the particular maladies referred to. Evidently the visual evidence of disease provided the primary basis for their identification. The close association in v. 27 of specific afflictions with Egypt reflects experience of the unpleasant conditions of the Nile delta. This fact forms a useful medical background to understanding the importance of the plague tradition of Exod. 7–12 and its association with that country. The story of Israel's deliverance under Moses was not simply one of gaining freedom from political oppression, but also a path to healing and protection. The personal misfortunes of a youth described in v. 30 recall closely the concessions granted in time of war in 20. 5–7.

The reference to *the king whom you have appointed* (v. 36) appears to make direct allusion to the circumstances of the arrest, imprisonment and exile of Jehoiachin in 598 BCE (cf. II Kgs. 24. 15). The emphasis on human choice in the phrase challenges the older belief that Israel's kings were chosen and appointed by God. Throughout Deuteronomy disillusionment with kingship, even that of the royal house of David, provides a powerful undercurrent which looked to Moses and the law in preference to David. The close links between the royal house of David and the city of Jerusalem had encouraged the belief that this city was an impregnable fortress which could be relied on to provide a sure defence against any enemy. The events of the sixth century BCE had shown the dangers of such false trust (cf. Lam 2. 1, 7; 4. 12). The threats of death and destruction in vv. 45–46 convey an atmosphere of finality, which is only partly softened by the warning that the future descendants of Israel will look back on the terrible fate of that particular generation, seeing in it a special sign (v. 46). The two verses bring the first list of curses to a conclusion, summarizing the reason for their terrible consequences.

A new section begins in v. 47 and continues as far as v. 57 in recalling specific instances of recent misfortune which had impressed their horror indelibly on the minds of Israel's people. The familiar speech-form of the curse as such, which is well preserved in 27. 14–26, is now completely abandoned, being replaced with a simple narrative forewarning of punishments that will be inflicted on the nation. Yet this feature of a forewarning is essentially didactic and rhetorical, since the experiences that are reported are undoubtedly those that overtook Judah in the first two decades of the sixth century when the old kingdom finally collapsed. For the reader they were a recent memory; some had experienced them personally and others had listened in awestruck fear to reports of what had taken place. What wrongdoing could lead to such enormities? This was the question which the author seeks to answer.

The opening line in v. 47 swiftly passes sentence upon the people for their disobedience already shown, moving on in the following verses to outline the punishment that the sentence merits. The focus then turns in vv. 52–57 to the horrors of a city enduring a prolonged siege, with extremes of hunger leading to cases of cannibalism (vv. 53, 55, 57). That some persons had lapsed into such behaviour in the distress of famine is reflected in several Old Testament passages (cf. Lev. 26. 29; Jer. 19. 9; Lam. 2. 20; 4. 10; Ezek. 5. 10). The terrible events of Jerusalem's endurance of a prolonged siege in the years 588–587 BCE, before succumbing to eventual surrender, are in the author's mind. The recalling of the events in such detail follows closely the echoing of similar themes in Lamentations. Their inclusion as a part of the epilogue to the Deuteronomic lawbook serves as an attempt to highlight yet further the necessity for obedience to the law.

The final section of the long list of curses (vv. 58–68) presents a summarizing review of the purpose of the entire book of Deuteronomy, shedding light on the central role it was intended to serve. Overall these additions to the list of the blessings and curses of God's covenant are highly distinctive on account of their explicit references to Deuteronomy as a book (v. 58; cf. also v. 61). Since the general outline form of Deuteronomy is that of a speech delivered by Moses the transition to recognizing its written literary form marks a significant step in the emergence of the concept of a 'Bible' – a book which discloses the way and will of God.

Once again the central focus on diseases as a punishment inflicted by God (vv. 59–61) is strikingly evident here. It undoubtedly reflects a popular and widespread understanding of their origin and purpose which has continued to the present day in popular thinking. In theological pespective Deuteronomy leans very heavily upon the concepts of divine justice and retribution as a means of understanding life in general and the history of Israel in particular. It is for this reason especially that the editing of the books of I and II Kings has been described as 'Deuteronomistic'. The limitations of such a perspective became increasingly evident in the light of later reflection and Israel's own experience. Within the Old Testament the book of Job is the greatest monument to this call for deeper reflection on the problem of disease in particular and of evil in general. Deuteronomy sets out a black and white proposition, which human experience has shown fails to reflect adequately the relationship of God to the natural world and to natural evils and misfortunes.

Verse 63 highlights very clearly the situation of Jerusalem after the siege and fall of the city in 587 BCE. This catastrophe brought about a period of political, social and religious turmoil such as Israel had not previously known. The land on which the nation had grown up came to be regarded as ruined and lost. All eyes eventually turned for hope

125

of renewal to those who had survived by seeking refuge among the nations, and especially the group who had earlier been deported to Babylon (see especially chapters 40–55 of the book of Isaiah). So the faithful of Israel came to be regarded as living in 'exile' among the nations, and hope turned to focus on the expectation of their return to rebuild the land.

The warning (v. 64) that Israel would *serve other gods* in its enforced exile among the nations represents the eventuality that the Deuteronomic authors most greatly feared, and which they sought most urgently to prevent happening. Tradition, contemporary convention, and the very desire to 'be like the nations round about' inevitably exerted immense pressure upon persons living in exile for this to happen. To settle down and begin a new life appeared necessarily to require the adoption of the gods worshipped in the new land of residence. Only the possession of 'the book of the law', with its focus on the past and the unique leadership of Moses, could prevent such a surrender of faith. The epilogue to Deuteronomy openly accepts that such a period of 'exile' among the nations now awaited Israel.

Events had shown the nation to be disobedient to God and the time for punishment had come. In line with this understanding, it is important to note how Deuteronomy fulfilled a mammoth theological task in refocusing the central beliefs of Israel's faith to enable it to survive the trials of this uncertain future. That Judaism has survived to become the faith of a worldwide community owes an immeasurable debt to this Deuteronomic reminting of a faith in God that embraced awareness of Israel's tragic past and made credible a hope for its future.

The descriptions of life as refugees seeking protection and temporary shelter (vv. 65–67) shows a remarkable empathy with an experience which has been echoed all too frequently in modern times. If hope is to be credible, it has to face the truth about the present. The concluding very pointed description in v. 68 of refugees returning to Egypt and freely offering themselves to be sold as slaves marks an ironic completion of a kind of 'circle of destiny' in the thinking of the Deuteronomic authors. They discerned a tragic cycle of promise, betrayal and punishment from which there was only one road of escape – renewed obedience to the covenant law of God! The speech that follows as Moses' farewell oration takes up this theme with an evangelical fervour. It message is: 'choose life and freedom by the only path that is open!'

In 29. 1 the choice between blessing or curse that faced Israel is presented as a consequence of the *terms of the covenant* made in the plains of Horeb. This covenant is here specifically declared to be additional to that which had earlier been made on Mount Horeb. It is surprising that, at this point, the idea of a further covenant is introduced into the book since its terms in no way differ from those of the covenant made on Mount Horeb. It is essentially a renewal and reaffirmation of the primary covenant by which Israel had become the people of the LORD God. The reason for renewal at this point lies in the recognition that Israel had reached a significant turning-point in its story: after thirty-eight years of wandering, it now found itself waiting to enter the land and to begin the great adventure of life under God's law. Israel's initial response to the covenant had been made, rather falteringly, under the watchful eye of Moses: a new phase was about to begin when Moses would no longer be their guardian and keeper and only the law he had bequeathed them would be their guide.

In larger theological perspective the idea of renewing and reaffirming the covenant with God was important, since it left open the assurance that, in spite of past failures, the covenant could be renewed and a new beginning made.

Moses' farewell speech
29. 2–30. 20

The contribution of Moses towards the formation, leadership and faith of Israel is now brought to a climactic conclusion with a farewell address which employs all the skills and artistry of persuasion that the ancient author had at his command. It is truly a masterpiece among the many important speeches contained in the Bible, offering a retrospect on Israel's experience of God, with many lessons learned. It explores every argument to show why Israel can look to the future with hope. Its brilliance lies in its probing beneath the surface of the working of the human mind, noting how people reason to themselves, excusing bad actions, and the reasons why a perceptive self-interest can lead them to make good decisions. In its second part it surveys the present state of Israel and looks to the future, exploring the significance of hope as an essential driving force of human identity and necessary for generating a sense of self-worth. Without hope the very foundations of personal identity crumble and only its recovery can offer a remedy for despair.

From a historical perspective it is evident that this farewell address is unlikely to have originated with the person of Moses himself, since the contemporary scene which it surveys is so clearly that which faced Israel in the twilight years of the sixth century. Jerusalem lay in ruins, its temple was destroyed and many of the population had been scattered, either fleeing to escape death or as a result of enforced deportation to distant lands. Moses speaks to all such persons, whether they were striving to survive in the land, or looking for a future return to their former homeland. To all of them he offers the lifeline of hope.

Since the twentieth century has witnessed so many comparable instances of national disaster, its contemporary relevance is not hard to find. However, the power of Moses' farewell speech lies not so much in its ability to address a particular historical situation but more in its uncovering of the deep-rooted human need for hope, exploring its theological roots in a manner that no other biblical passage does. It looks squarely at the reasons for despair and counters them with God's assurance. Its key text is presented at the end with a remarkable intensity of feeling: *Choose life and you and your descendants will live* (30. 19).

In its structure the speech falls into two distinct parts, the first of which, in 29. 2–29, looks back over the past, bringing Israel's story up to date in much the same manner that a father might review the story of his family to the time when it breaks up and goes on separate paths. The second part, in 30. 1–20, looks to the future as a time of new beginnings. The unknown remainder of Israel's story is about to commence and the grounds of hope are set out. Not only is the rebuilding of the land with its towns and cities possible, but this will only happen if it is preceded by the rebuilding of individual lives through penitence and courage. The appropriateness of reflecting on the situation when the nation's pioneers had been about to march across the Jordan to enter the land for the first time is easy to see.

The speech of Moses divides clearly into two major sections, the first of which (in 29. 2–29) sets out a review of the past. There is an understandable touch of artistic licence in the assertion: *You have seen for yourselves* . . . (v. 2). The generation that had witnessed events in Egypt had rebelled against Moses and died in the wilderness. Nevertheless the story of the humiliation of Egypt's Pharaoh was fully known and its truth acknowledged. What was lacking was a grasp of the implications of this experience (v. 4). The Hebrew for *mind* is literally 'heart' as the organ through which understanding occurs

128

(v. 4). There is a deliberate touch of irony designed to prompt deeper reflection and compel a changed attitude of mind; cf. similarly Isa. 6. 10. The reference to Israel's experience in the wilderness (v. 5; cf. 8. 2–4) is made in order to show that God could be wholly trusted to look after basic human needs. The events regarding the kings Sihon and Og (v. 7) are recounted in 2. 31–33 and the Deuteronomic continued interest in the Transjordanian lands is renewed in v. 8. This was a region which had been lost to Greater Israel from an early period, but Deuteronomy regarded it still as an essential part of the 'ideal' Israel.

The differing social status of each of the groups that made up the nation is well reflected in vv. 10–11. Performance of the most servile tasks was a mark of inferiority and carried with it a stigma of humiliation cf. Jos. 9. 27. Those who were aliens represent a marginalized section of the community to which the Deuteronomic authors were repeatedly concerned to draw attention. However weak their position within the national life may have become, they were nevertheless members of the community of God. Accordingly this theological inclusiveness marked a major step in addressing a deep-rooted social problem.

A central feature of the covenant-making ceremony referred to in v. 13 was the performance of a solemn oath affirming loyalty and obedience. Overall the book of Deuteronomy interprets the covenant-oath sworn to the nation's ancestors (cf. Gen. 15. 1–20) as a promise leading to the covenant of Horeb (5. 1–3), and the covenant made in the plains of Moab as a renewal of this Horeb covenant (cf. 29. 1 and comments there). So the covenants are interrelated and do not involve different terms. The reference in v. 15 to *those who are not here with us today* is to future generations who would be born into this covenant relationship with the LORD God.

A further effort at showing up the folly of idolatry appears in vv. 16–21 with the mention of the idols which existed in Egypt. The imaginative description of the numerous images, many of massive size, that were to be found there both reflects a knowledge of that land, and more particularly of the many, often hugely impressive, idols and religious images of the lands to which scattered Judean citizens would flee. In this way idol-worship was linked with all that was objectionable and oppressive in the foreign powers that had treated Israel so cruelly. The temptation to follow the conventions and practices of those who worshipped in these foreign lands (v. 19) must undoubtedly have represented the major temptation for scattered Jewish exiles. The belief that gods were themselves territorially based

129

as 'gods of the land' was widespread and the traditional Jewish places of worship, especially Jerusalem, had become inaccessible to many would-be loyal Jews. It would have appeared easier to seek the help of the gods who were at hand, than to cling to the worship of a God who seemed far off. The processes by which Jews, exiled into foreign lands, resisted their new religious environment can only be traced with difficulty. In countering the inevitable temptations, and in recognition of the deep-rooted impulse to faith and prayer in every human being, Jews introduced new forms of assembly for prayer, which eventually led to the building of synagogues and a simplified form of worship which served as a kind of distant adjunct to that of the temple in Jerusalem.

The references to Deuteronomy as a book, in vv. 20–21, 27, highlight the remarkable way in which the book reveals an awareness of its own literary significance. It was to be used for public reading and reflection and was destined itself to become a central feature of the new pattern of worship by which Israel's life among the nations would become bearable and faith-filled. The remnants of the nation were to become the people of a book which formed the indispensable guide to show how God remained accessible. It was the vital key to understanding the origin and terms of God's covenant. Reading from it provided what has become the essential basis for both Jewish and Christian worship ever since.

In vv. 22–28 the poem reviews the devastated condition of the land as a consequence of the calamities that would overtake Israel. The descriptive detail shows clearly that the authors were well aware they were pointing to a reality that had already become a recent fact. The ruination of the land is graphically described, providing an informative picture of the deliberate actions to render it useless and infertile, consequent upon the military campaign which brought about Jerusalem's destruction. Such measures were aimed at preventing the redevelopment of a region as punishment for breach of treaty obligations.

The four cities of Sodom, Gomorrah, Admah and Zeboyim (v. 23) are also mentioned together in Gen. 10. 19; 14. 2, 8, and the story of how Sodom and Gomorrah were destroyed under God's judgement is narrated in Gen. 19. As cities whose downfall acquired a proverbial significance these two are referred to further in Amos 4. 11; Isa. 1. 9; 13. 19) while Admah and Zeboyim are referred to in Hos. 11. 8.

The question that is put into the mouths of future generations (v. 24) was one that was undoubtedly already being asked by the book's readers. The boldness of the answer in v. 25 was a pivotal feature of the rationale of Deuteronomy. Even the most dire human tragedy is not left without explanation. The mention in v. 28 that God's punishment had resulted in the people of Israel being banished to another land reflects the lateness of this part of the Deuteronomic epilogue. Such a dispersion of a nation into exile, as comprehensively viewed, was already taking place. All hope of renewing normal life among the survivors in Judah had collapsed and now only hope of a return from this exile provided a realistic plan for the future.

The meaning of v. 29 is that, although there are many truths about the nature and reality of God which cannot be known, there are nevertheless certain essential truths which relate to human existence which are known. They are to be found written in the book of God's law. In this way the objection that God's ways are always filled with mystery and cannot be grasped by the human intellect, is countered by insisting that the truths that really matter for human beings are known. Essentially the same point is made further in 30. 11–14. God indeed is mysterious in the whole range of what Godhead means, but such a mystery must not be taken to imply that human beings cannot know anything at all about divinity. God chooses to reveal what is essential for human beings to know.

The second part of Moses' speech turns to the question of hope for the future (30. 1–20). The situation in which the reader is assumed to be placed is openly made perfectly clear by the recognition that the painful events of which they had been forewarned had already occurred.This is implicit in the opening admonition (30. 1): *When all these things have happened to you, the blessing and the curse* . . . Disaster had by this time already stricken the land which the readers loved. It lay before them in ruins so it was already too late to prevent disaster and to avert the consequences of the curses. But it was not too late to shape a different future. It is this prospect to which the speech now turns. That many of the book's readers were already assumed to be living in exile among the nations is freely brought into the reckoning. The question was what hope was there of any eventual return to the land which had been lost.

So a very great deal hinges on the conditional declaration of v. 2: *If you and your children turn back to him*. . . It is one of the most forceful invitations to repentance that the Old Testament contains. The conditions for restoration and a new life in the land are held to be straightforward enough. They are that every Israelite should first return inwardly to God in heart and mind, before there can be an outward

131

physical return to the land which had been promised to Israel's ancestors. It is a declaration of hope which gives shape and purpose to the entire Old Testament as a canon of Scripture. No one is a prisoner of the past, since God always holds out an invitation to share a different future. It is this message, and the prospect of what it will bring with it, which occupies the remainder of the poem.

The description given of Israel's situation, in what is now openly recognized as the inglorious present of exile among the nations (v. 5), is a situation which can never be robbed of hope. This hope becomes of central importance for understanding the way in which the Hebrew Bible as a whole is built up around the twin themes of law and promise. By heeding the words of God's law the way to secure the promised future becomes clear. The metaphor of a circumcision of the heart (v. 6) has already been used in 10. 16. Here the act of such a spiritual circumcision is said to be performed by God himself so that acceptance into the covenant is made into an act of divine empowering. The idea finds a close parallel in Jer. 31. 31–34 (cf. Ezek. 11. 19; 36. 26–27). That God would change the mentality of Israel so as to ensure future obedience to the covenant sweeps aside the objection that the future could turn out to be like the past. If the covenant placed upon Israel the responsibility of choice, what assurance was there that the people would choose the path of obedience? The counter-argument presented here insists that God will so rejoice over Israel that the power to respond will be given to the people. It is a message that is almost Pauline in its audacity.

The argument of vv. 6–10 comes close to the classical formulations of the arguments of the priority of grace over law that have had strong echoes in Christian tradition. Now a rather different argument is presented concerning the very nature of God's revelation. What is demanded of Israel is not an unfulfillable catalogue of demands which can never be wholly met. God's law is clear and plain for all to know and understand, since it is openly and freely available to all. It exists in a book, and it is the goal of Deuteronomy to set forth the requirements of this law with the utmost clarity, to warn of the temptations which might lead to its neglect, and to ensure that it was accessible to all future generations. For those who followed the instructions of 6. 6–9 the law would be as familiar as breathing itself.

The starkness of the choice that faces Israel is set forth with passionate force and clarity in v. 15. It is a straightforward decision between life and survival, or death and oblivion. The concluding appeal in vv. 19–20 reverberates with a sense that a moment of crisis and choice now exists which cannot be ignored and which will not return again. Everything that the future promised is seen to hinge on the necessity for making the right choice. *Today I offer you the choice. . .* It is a Gospel invitation.

The death of Moses and the preservation of the law book 31. 1–34. 12

There now follow a series of appendices which bring the book to a conclusion and which narrate the story of Moses' death and the provision made for the future of the law book. The primary focus rests on the circumstances of Moses' death before he had set foot in the land and the transfer of leadership to Joshua. Into these narrative details two extended poems, the Song of Moses (31. 30–32. 44) and the Blessing of Moses (33. 1–29), have been inserted in order to complete the collection of Moses' literary bequest to the nation. Altogether the various poems and narratives do not appear to have originated at the same time, but to have been introduced in stages, reflecting the later literary history of Deuteronomy as a book.

The Song of Moses is introduced in vv. 16–22, but this unit interrupts the account of how Joshua was installed as Moses' successor in vv. 14–15, 23. Verses 24–29 then create a further break between the song and its introduction by giving instructions for preserving the book of the law beside the Ark of the Covenant. This unevenness in the literary sequence reflects the history through which the incorporation of the book of Deuteronomy into the biblical canon has taken place. Originally the law book was connected directly to the historical books of Joshua–Judges–I and II Samuel–I and II Kings (often referred to by scholars as the 'Deuteronomistic History', on account of this link with Deuteronomy). A subsequent restructuring has separated the law book from this history and incorporated Deuteronomy as the last of the five books of Moses. It thereby completes the present Pentateuch (Genesis to Deuteronomy) as five books of 'law' for the guidance for every Jew whether living in the land or scattered among the nations. This has brought about an element of repetition in the accounts of the handing over of leadership from Moses to Joshua in Deut. 31. 7–8, 14–15 and Jos. 1. 1–9. Two major themes are present in these appended reports: the first affirms that the giving of God's law, by which Israel must henceforth live, is now complete and the second reports that God has appointed Joshua as the successor to Moses. Seen

133

in the further context of the book of Joshua this transfer of leadership paves the way for the eventual introduction of a monarchy.

Preparations for life without Moses
31. 1–13

The anticipation of his own imminent death required that three steps be taken by Moses (vv. 1–2). The first is to make a brief, military-style, exhortation to the people to take courage and begin the great adventure that awaited them on the other side of the Jordan (vv. 3–6); the second step is to summon Joshua and to indicate that the burden of leadership of the nation will now fall upon his shoulders (vv. 7–8). The third step is to make provision for the preservation and public reading of the laws which he had declared (vv. 9–13). Without the presence of Moses life would be lived under a new order in which the book of the Mosaic law, rather than the physical presence and leadership of the great man, would govern the lives of the people. So even the new style of leadership would be different, since the new leader would be required first and foremost to ensure that the law was made known and observed (cf. 17. 18–20).

The recognition that Moses would *not cross the Jordan* (v. 2) possessed a deep symbolic significance for the people. By the time Deuteronomy was complete as a book many of Israel's most devoted former citizens also found themselves, like Moses, on the wrong side of the Jordan and outside the promised land. The world of dispersion and exile had begun. The book of the law was addressed to every Jew, whether living in the former Israel, or forced to reside among alien nations, as Moses had forewarned (28. 64–68; 29. 28). Many would now be compelled to share the experience of looking to the land only as a place of future promise, and not of fulfilment. Yet life without Moses did not mean life without God, for God's presence would accompany the people and Joshua's leadership would continue something at least of the tradition that Moses had begun (v. 3). Even in the face of its own military weakness, Israel could therefore still be strong (for the parable-like significance of the victories over Sihon and Og see 29. 7–8).

The theme of God's accompanying presence to lead Israel into battle (v. 6; cf. also v. 8 below) does not fit altogether smoothly with the strong emphasis upon God's dwelling place in heaven (cf. 26. 15) and the insistence that only the approved place for a sanctuary is where God's name has been set (cf. 12. 11). In most respects the

134

traditional language of the divine presence with Israel has been submitted to careful reflection and re-examination by the Deuteronomists in the light of the disasters which had befallen many of Israel's former holy places. Cf. also 31. 8.

It is noteworthy that in v. 7 Moses takes the initiative to seek out Joshua as his successor, whereas in vv. 14–15 it is God who first gives instructions for Joshua's appointment. Furthermore in v. 23 the emphasis upon God's choice and commissioning of Joshua is paramount. Human initiative and divine empowering are seen to be part of one consistent purpose. The terms of the commissioning are markedly stereotyped, strongly suggesting that they reflect the established wording of a ceremony for installation to a public office.

The transfer of leadership in the imminent prospect of Moses' death (v. 8), is presented as a major turning-point in the history of the entire nation. This ultimately focuses primarily on the existence of the law book, which is the basis for human leadership to continue what Moses had begun. Eventually the question of leadership in battle, and the sense that it had been lacking, was to bring about the demand for a king (cf. I Sam. 8. 1–22). So a form of human succession is envisaged by Deuteronomy which began with Moses and carried on through Joshua and the judges, until David's kingship offered a fresh period of hope. Yet this also had now to be regarded as belonging to a past era, creating an urgent need to look back to the beginning to discern afresh in Moses those qualities which displayed God's power and will.

The great attention to Moses' quality as a leader throughout Deuteronomy reflects this sense that the kingship, even that of David's dynasty, had proved to be a disappointment. The strong attention to Moses' death outside the land, reflects this consciousness that this event marked an irreversible turning-point. Only obedience to the Mosaic law book could serve to recover a knowledge of all that Moses had meant! No other leader – not even king David – measured up to his stature (cf. 34. 10).

The inadequacy of human leadership to measure up to the stature of Moses is compensated for in another way altogether by the law book, for the future of which provision has now to be made (vv. 9–13). Accordingly, the primary role of the levitical priests would in future be that of serving as custodians of the book of the law. This strongly suggests that they also were to become teachers of the law. At first this appears as a subordinate, and largely ancillary duty, but when the changed political situation of Israel is taken into account the relative priorities also quickly changed. For Jews living apart from *the place*

135

which the LORD *God will choose to set his name there* the teaching of the law was the primary means of retaining a continuity with the land and the ideals which had been learnt in the land.

That the law was read (v. 10), at least in part, during the Feast of Booths (Tabernacles) was reflected in later Jewish worship by focusing attention during that festival on the giving of the law on Mount Horeb (Sinai). The instruction that this was to take place once every seven years is surprising since the interval is far too great for it to have provided a meaningful educational opportunity. The law itself called for reflection upon it daily in every home (cf. 6. 7). The action here can only have been intended as a symbolic ceremonial upholding of the law as a focus of national life. The selection of readings from it (v. 11), as the central focus of worship, became an inescapable consequence of the place acccorded to it in Deuteronomy. In turn it brought about a fundamental shift in the character of worship. This became first and foremost an act of revitalizing human understanding of God and of recovering awareness of the divine will for humankind. This reordering of the basic requirements of worship, as set out in vv. 12–13, eventually led to its shaping the worship practised in synagogues into modern times.

Providing for the future
  31. 14–29

The sequence of events in the narrative which recounts the last days of Moses is broken up by the introduction to the poetic Song of Moses in vv. 10–22, 30. This has become detached from the arrangements made for the religious leadership of Israel after the death of Moses. The incidents recounted include God's commissioning of Joshua (31. 14–15, 23), the instruction for placing the book of the law beside the holy Ark of the Covenant (31. 24–26) and the giving of final warnings concerning the temptations that will come to abandon the exclusive worship of the LORD as God (31. 16–18, 27–29). The dangerous nature and inevitability of this temptation provide their own introduction to the song which Moses is about to give. There is a sense of near inescapable tragedy in the words of v. 29 *In days to come disaster will befall you . . .* The readers of the book would know all too well how justified this warning had been.

The making of the Tent of Meeting referred to in v. 14 is described in Exod. 33. 7–11 and Joshua's regular presence there noted. The signifying of God's presence at the Tent of Meeting in the form of a

136

cloud (v. 15) is reported in Exod. 33. 10–11. This strongly suggests that the cloud was itself a feature of the ceremonies conducted in the tent, almost certainly related to the use of incense. From the account of its origin in Exod. 33 the tent was especially important for the receiving of oracles. The purpose of the cloud appears twofold, on the one hand indicating that God, who is the 'Rider of the Clouds' (cf. Ps. 18. 9–10) could appear to human beings, but also signifying that the full divine form could never be seen by human eyes but must remain hidden (cf. Exod. 33. 1–9). The reference made in v. 16 to living among foreigners is noteworthy in view of the command that they should be exterminated (7. 2). However, the author's awareness has clearly carried forward to reflect on the prospect that awaited many of the people who would be forced to live among the nations as a result of their disobedience. These citizens would now face as great a period of temptation to turn to other gods as any that had previously confronted Israel. *Will wantonly worship their gods* is more literally rendered in NRSV 'will begin to prostitute themselves to the foreign gods . . .'

The metaphor of the 'hiding' of God's face (v. 17) is frequently used in the Psalms as an expression for God's refusal to hear prayer and to come to the aid of the worshipper. The inference here is that, what the people misinterpret as God's absence will come about because they have angered God, who no longer listens to them. The references in vv. 17–18 to *on that day* undoubtedly have in mind the time of Judah's downfall, when every prayer for God's help appeared to be unavailing. Cf. Lam. 3. 8. The theme of turning to other gods prepares for the Song of Moses, where it is dealt with more extensively. The contrast between Moses' obedience and the people's disobedience (v. 19) has already been established as a major theme concerning the years spent in the wilderness. The refusal to heed God's warnings leads to wasted years of life.

It is a repeated and perceptive Deuteronomic theme that prosperity and times of plenty will prove to be a greater, and more subtle temptation, than times of hardship and deprivation (v. 20). Living on the bare essentials in the wilderness years had taught Israel to be conscious of its dependence on God's provision whereas times of prosperity and success in agriculture encouraged forgetfulness of this. The basis of foreknowledge of future disaster (vv. 17, 21) was not because it was already fixed and predetermined, but because Moses knew the subtle and devious workings of the human mind! Such insight accords well with the ancient Greek maxim 'Know thyself!' (cf. 31. 27).

Joshua would be a leader 'like Moses' (v. 23; cf. also Jos. 1. 5–7), but with one essential difference. Moses had given the law, Joshua needed to read it and think about it constantly (Jos. 1. 8). The writing down of the law referred to in v. 24 contrasts with Deut. 1. 3–5; 4. 45 where Moses proclaims the law to the Israelites in a speech. The transition to the written recording of the laws in a book reflects a very significant development, both in legal practice (the making of law books, or codes), and in the emergence of a 'Bible' (a collection of books to form a guide to life in covenant with God). The use of writing and written documentation as a primary feature of faith and obedience was increasingly to shape the religious future. Judaism, Christianity and Islam are the three great monotheistic faiths of humankind – each of them 'the religion of a book'.

For the placing in the Ark of the Covenant of the two tablets with the Ten Commandments written on them cf. 10. 3–5. These commandments and the longer law book of Deuteronomy were not two different laws, but the shorter and longer editions of the one great law of the covenant between Israel and the LORD God. The sense of the inevitability of disaster is repeated in v. 29 from vv. 17, 21, 27. Judgement is not predetermined by God, but by the stubbornness and defiance of the human heart (so especially v. 27). From the author's temporal perspective such disasters had already become a reality. What was needed was an explanation for them showing that they had not been inevitable but had happened because Israel had provoked God's anger. Israel's defiant indifference to God's law had aroused the divine wrath, just as it had provoked Moses to anger centuries before.

The Song of Moses
31. 30–32. 44

The Song of Moses appears as a distinctive, and relatively independent, composition which has been inserted into the law book of Deuteronomy at a late stage. Its connection with the book lies in its message of accusation and challenge addressed to Israel, with a timeless warning that the temptation to disobedience and idolatry will remain a continuing one. Knowing God's law is one part of the way of faith, the other part lies in learning obedience to it. This can only be achieved by constant watchfulness and self-examination, which is the challenge of the message that the Song presents.

The Song itself is contained in 32. 1–43 and falls into two parts.

138

Verses 1–25 are set out in the form of a lawsuit, detailing the charges brought against Israel, the evidence for them and pronouncing the sentence that the inevitable guilty verdict has deserved. The second part, in vv. 26–43, then reflects further on this, with God weighing up the consequences that the deserved punishment will bring and examining reasons why this cannot be the final outcome. Other considerations must also be brought into the reckoning.

The Song is formally introduced in 31. 30 and its conclusion is noted in 32. 44. The first part has close parallels in a number of prophetic passages, where God prosecutes a case against Israel (cf. especially Isa. 1; Jer. 2; Mic. 6; Ps. 50). The second part is more reflective and abandons the form of a lawsuit to find its nearest counterparts in the arguments and discourses of the wisdom tradition, most readily seen in the book of Ecclesiastes. Although therefore the first part is sharply accusatory of Israel and its disloyalty to God, the second part turns the theme of judgement into one of hope. Necessary and justifiable as God's judgement upon human failure may be, grace is stronger than wrath and hope will triumph over despair. God's power as Creator implies the divine will for human redemption.

The Song was evidently not original to the Deuteronomic authors, but its time of composition can most probably be set in the middle of the sixth century BCE. God's warnings of judgement had been expounded and explored sufficiently fully to account for the failures of the past. The task now was to rebuild and this called for a reasoned and honest look at the possibilities of hope for the future. The physical rebuilding of the land could only occur after an inward spiritual rebuilding of a reasoned hope. A careful examination of the various modern translations, with their marginal notes, indicates that the text of the Song is often unclear.

The appeal to the heavens and the earth (v. 1) is that they may serve as witnesses to the case that is now to be presented. The charges are clearly presented and the witnesses are to acknowledge this (vv. 1–3). The case that is to be considered is now declared in vv. 4–6. God the Creator is faithful and just, but the people who are his children have shown themselves foolish and senseless. The charges are now set out in greater detail in vv. 7–14, stretching back to the time of Israel's creation as a nation and the period of its origins in the wilderness.

The Hebrew text of v. 8 reads 'sons of Israel' instead of 'sons of God', but the latter must undoubtedly be the original correct sense. The concern to remove any apparent conflict with monotheism has led to the alteration when the tradition that other gods exist as the

139

guardian deities of other nations was seen to stand in conflict with it. Later scribes have imposed a stricter understanding of monotheism. The teaching of verse 8 is that, in the beginning, the Most High God allocated to each nation its own patron deity. Verse 9 then insists that the LORD chose Israel as a people to watch over, with the understanding that the titles 'Most High' and 'LORD' are alternative titles of the one God of Israel. The short poetic passage has adapted the ancient tradition of many gods, arranged in a hierarchy, in order to show the supremacy of the one LORD God of Israel. Throughout Deuteronomy there is a 'practical monotheism' which is nevertheless hesitant to deny that other gods exist for other nations. The central feature is that they are inferior deities who cannot thwart the will of the God of Israel. To what extent this 'seeming existence' of other gods for other nations had any reality was later examined more critically (cf. also Ps. 96. 4–5).

The LORD God is presented as the special Divine Guardian of Israel (v. 9), but this interpretation of a 'national' deity was later modified in Jewish thought to the belief that the guardian patrons of nations were leading angelic figures (cf. Dan. 12. 1 with 10. 13). The belief that Israel's origin as a people was in the wilderness (v. 10) is in line with the portrait of the nation's ancestor as 'a wandering Aramaean' (26. 5). The reference is not specifically to the forty years spent wandering in the desert after the escape from slavery in Egypt, but to the whole way of life of the ancestors from whom the nation had sprung. The important point is that, at that time, they possessed no land of their own. That only the LORD God alone was worshipped by them at that time (v. 12) was a practical step towards monotheism which has sometimes been described as monolatry. The First Commandment developed this in precluding the worship of any god beside (or 'alongside') the LORD God of Israel (5. 7).

In vv. 13–14 the imagery of the fertile productivity of the land is contrasted with the *howling waste* of the desert (v. 10). That grape harvests and wine were the products of the settled agricultural land. That it also held dangers was widely recognized; cf. Gen. 9. 20–25. The refusal of certain groups to take wine marked a desire to retain the discipline of the older, harsher, conditions of desert life; cf. Jer. 35. 1–11. Civilization and an improved 'standard of living' came at a cost which some were not prepared to pay. The title *Jeshurun* of v. 15 is a rarely used title for Israel, which appears again in 33. 5, 26; Isa. 44. 2. If it is to be associated with the verb meaning 'to be straight, upright', then a deliberate play on words is intended. The 'upright one' has been easily seduced by luxury! The imagery of the rich possibilities of life in the settled agricultural land, when compared with the conditions of the desert, reflect a very deep rooted and traditional contempt for luxury felt by the half-nomad populations of the region which has continued into the present day.

In v. 16 the *abominable practices* are literally 'abhorrent things', using the same noun which describes a number of illegal, or reprehensible, actions condemned in the law code. Deuteronomy sees an inseparable link between bad religion and bad behaviour. The term *demons* of v. 17 refers to the older gods of the land and is used again in Ps. 106. 37 where it is linked to human child sacrifices (cf. also 32. 17). Their horrific demands shows that they cannot be true 'gods'. The claim that these gods were *strangers to them* implies that they had had no historical connection with Israel's past. It was a very basic assumption of the Canaanite deities that they were 'gods of the land'; i.e. they 'owned', and brought life-giving fertility, to the land which Israel farmed. The offering of sacrifices (?even human sacrifices) formed the payment to these gods of their due. Accordingly agriculture and 'strange gods' were linked together in the popular mind so that even farming routines possessed a ritual accompaniment (cf. Ps. 126. 5–6).

In v. 18 the NRSV reads more literally 'You were unmindful of the Rock that bore you', but the Hebrew is difficult and the REB's *You forsook the Creator who begot you* gives the more probable sense. The *people of no account* referred to in v. 21 is literally a 'no people'. The identity of such a non-Israelite community is unclear, and no precise definition is likely to have been in mind. It is a case where 'the punishment fits the crime' – Israel had worshipped foreign gods, and so would be punished by a foreign people; for the idea cf. Isa. 5. 26–30 – a passage which may be alluded to here. The Sheol referred to in v. 22 was thought of as the abode to which the dead were taken and was considered as a subterranean world. It frequently occurs in expressions denoting extremes of depth (cf. Isa. 7. 11). For the metaphor of fire as God's judgement cf. Amos 7. 4.

For the *ravages of plague* (cf. NRSV 'burning consumption') referred to in v. 24 it is noteworthy that the noun 'plague' that is used is that of a deity in Ugaritic (Canaanite) texts.

The mood and purpose of the Song changes significantly at verse 26. All that has preceded has made vigorous poetic use of the theme that Israel's misfortunes and political disasters are the consequence of God's judgements. The trial is over and sentence has been passed. The justice of this judgement is not denied, but the further development of

141

the Song explores the recognition that it is not, and cannot be, the whole truth about God and the divine purpose for Israel.

We can look to Isa. 10. 13–15 for the idea that for an enemy to boast of a victory over Israel that God had given (v. 27) was an act of gross presumption. In turn the agent of God's judgement would be judged. The *nation* referred to in v. 28 is not named and the charge of foolishness is applied to Israel in verse 6. Yet the sense is better maintained if the nation referred to is not Israel, but the *foolish nation* who opposes Israel in v. 21. Vv. 28–29 then accuse Israel's enemies of failing to understand that their mission of judgement is limited and has been given them by God.

The implication of v. 30 must be that Israel's enemies have achieved great military successes, but only because God has willed that they should do so. Great military triumphs are a sure indication that they are given by God (cf. 28. 7, 25), who determines the outcome of every battle, even when it is an enemy's victory over the chosen people!

For the proverbial status of Sodom and Gomorrah (v. 32) as places under God's judgement we may compare 29. 23. Their mention here is not because they lay in ruins, but because of their proverbial corruption and immorality. So even their best gifts (v. 33) are a poisoned chalice. It is then an inevitable effect of the law of retribution that, in turn, the time will come for those who administered judgement to suffer it themselves (cf. Isa. 10. 12). The gods of the nations who had appeared so alluring, and so powerful when the nations who worshipped them appeared to be so successful, would then be shown to be nothing at all – mere figments of human imagination (v. 37). All the worship that was once offered to them would be shown to have been pointless. The affirmation of the complete and absolute sovereignty of God expressed in v. 39 closely mirrors the language of Isa. 45. 7 (cf. also Isa. 41. 4; 43. 10; 44. 6, 22; 48. 12).

The text of v. 43 reads rather strangely, since the appeal to the lesser gods in heaven to bow down in praise to the God of Israel, conflicts with the assertion that such supposed gods are really not gods at all (cf. vv. 21, 27). However, both the ancient Greek (Septuagint) and a Qumran Scroll tradition differ substantially from the standard Hebrew text. Several of the variants and additions are noted in the margin of REB. The underlying sense is that God has reserved judgement upon those nations which oppose Israel for an unspecified future day.

The Song is brought to a close in v. 44 with the presence of Joshua

142

and Moses seen together by all the people. Their relationship as leader and successor has now become an important feature for all Israel to observe. In its general outline the Song of Moses presents a review and a forecast of how Israel will fare under the new era created by the gift of the Mosaic law book. The final stages of the story still lie in the future.

From a distance
   32. 45–52

The ending of the Song of Moses calls for a further commendation of the law book and an opportunity for Moses to see from a distance the land which lay across the River Jordan. The sense of a parting of the ways is now made more prominent (v. 47), since Moses cannot share with his people the crossing into the land. Joshua will prove to be a useful leader, but only obedience to the law book can guarantee success and survival. Life after Moses will be significantly different from what it had been under his leadership. For Moses' ascent of Mount Nebo (v. 49) we can note the parallel account in Num. 27. 12. *Abarim* refers to the range of mountains in the territory of Moab, which lay east of the Dead Sea, and Nebo was its highest peak. According to Deut. 3. 27 the name of the mountain which Moses climbed to see the land was Mount Pisgah (cf. 34. 1) and according to 10. 6 the name of the mountain where Aaron died is Moserah. The name is given as Mount Hor in Num. 20. 22–29; 33. 37–39.

The accusation that Moses had 'broken faith' with God by his action at Meribath-kadesh (v. 51) appears surprising, since according to 3. 26 he was denied the privilege of crossing into the land solely as a result of the people's rebelliousness, not on account of any wrongdoing of his own. The report of what happened at Meribath-kadesh is given in Num. 20. 1–13 (usually ascribed to the late Priestly source). It is held against Moses that his question in Num. 20. 10 implied a lack of faith in God's holy power to effect a miracle (so Num. 20. 12). This is what is meant by the charge that he failed to uphold God's holiness among the Israelites. More generally Moses appears in biblical tradition as a leader who suffered unjustly on account of the sins of others. His burial place in the land of Moab is reported in 34. 6.

143

Moses' farewell blessing
33. 1–29

In keeping with the tradition that a father could impart a blessing to his children before his death, Moses now pronounces a blessing on all twelve of the tribes of Israel, who form his 'spiritual children'. A close parallel is to be found in the Blessing of Jacob in Gen. 49. 1–28 which also enumerates the twelve tribes. Comparable lists of these are also presented in Num. 1. 5–15 and 26. 5–62. Which tribes are included to make up the twelve differs slightly between the various lists, indicating that the retention of the number at twelve was important and that the status and vitality of individual tribes changed over time. The circumstances and details of these changes are often hinted at cryptically in the separate sayings, but the full circumstances can only be partially reconstructed.

It is in this context that this 'blessing' and that of Gen. 49 are especially interesting to the historian since they reveal that Israel's origins as a community made up of twelve tribes was an 'ideal', and rather artificial, portrait of the nation's origins. That all twelve tribes originated with twelve sons of one patriarchal ancestor – Jacob-Israel – is itself a reconstruction of a complex socio-political history. Such fragmentary insights as are given in these 'blessings' are invaluable towards understanding this history, but a full picture remains unobtainable.

The present Blessing of Moses represents one of the several appendices to Deuteronomy and was added at a late stage in the book's composition. As an independent poem, it appears probably to be of relatively early origin. We have noted that, in its overall political theology, Deuteronomy reckons with Israel as a 'nation' and it regards this national dimension as built up around four basic institutional pillars: ethnic origin (shared kinship), territory (the land promised to the ancestors), government (kingship of the royal dynasty chosen by God) and religion (exclusive worship of the LORD alone as God).

We have also noted, however, that behind this national dimension lies a far older awareness that Israel was a society based on ties of kinship in which extended family units (tribes, father's houses (clans), and individual households) were the structural units. In general Deuteronomy aims at injecting a sense of 'national' identity, with strong support for regional activities and responsibilities, even to the limiting of the authority of the heads of the large extended families who otherwise determined social and moral issues.

In the Blessing of Moses the gifts and graces of the named tribes are cryptically summarized and encapsulated in short sayings and word-images which serve to highlight their variety and individuality. These sayings appear in vv. 6–25, with vv. 1–5 and 26–29 providing a framework for them which celebrates the power and magnificence of God. It seems highly likely that this hymnic beginning and ending once constituted a separate composition and that the sayings regarding the tribes have simply been inserted into it. Taken overall they express a genuine delight in the variety and colourful panorama of human individuality.

The title *man of God* applied to Moses in v. 1 is frequently applied to prophets (I Kgs. 17. 18; II Kgs. 4. 7, 9) and is used again of Moses in the heading to Ps. 90 and Jos. 14. 6. The imminence of Moses' death lends a special sense of authority and power, since, at such a moment, the very life-spirit of the great man is felt to be imparted to those who receive his blessing.

The reference in 33. 2 is the only place in Deuteronomy where the mount of revelation is named *Sinai*; elsewhere in the book it is Horeb. The reference to the *myriads of holy ones* is puzzling. The Hebrew text avers that God came 'from', rather than 'with' them (cf. the marginal note in REB), and the comparable affirmation in Ps. 68. 17 suggests that he came 'to' or 'among' his holy ones (i.e. his people). The Hebrew text of v. 3 is obscure and has given rise to various attempts to reconstruct a probable original; cf. the differing modern versions and marginal notes. The following verse 4 appears as an attempt to clarify the meaning of this uncertain text by declaring that the law is God's great blessing for Israel.

For *Jeshurun* as a title of Israel (v. 5) cf. 32. 15. The reference to the king is unclear. It may be a reference to God who is 'King' over his people Israel. However, the lack of any reference to kingship arising from the tribe of Judah through David in v. 7 may suggest that this is the intended reference here.

33. 6 *Reuben* The introductory *Of Reuben he said* is missing in the text (cf. NRSV), but has been restored in REB to accord with the sayings concerning other tribes. In spite of Reuben being Jacob's firstborn son (Gen. 49. 32; 49. 3), his was a small tribe which plays no effective part in Israel's history. The wish for the tribe to be *few in number*, is very surprising and the sense is probably better conveyed by NRSV's 'even

though his numbers are few'. Gen. 49. 4 refers back to a sexual misdemeanour as the reason for this hostility and decline.

33. 7 *Judah* Judah's tribal territory was in the mountainous south and this isolation explains the call for God to join it to the other tribes. It is surprising that the rise of the Davidic kingship is not mentioned here, unless a reference to it is intended in v. 5 (cf. also Gen. 49. 10). Quite possibly the Deuteronomic distrust of the institution has called for a realignment, shifting the focus from the earthly to the divine king.

33. 8–11 *Levi* REB's rendering is based on the ancient Greek text. For the *Thummim* and *Urim* (usually in the reverse order) cf. Exod. 28. 30; Lev. 8. 8. These comprised a means (two marked stones?) for obtaining a divine oracle, which led to the involvement of the levitical priests in settling legal disputes. The testing at *Massah* and *Meribah* is recounted in Exod. 17. 1–7, where it is applicable to all Israel, and the Levites are not mentioned. Here it appears that the testing of Israel has been understood to mark a testing of Moses and Aaron, as representatives of the priesthood, in particular (cf. 32. 51).

The tradition that the Levites had shown themselves to be uncompromisingly loyal to the LORD as God asserted in v. 9 refers to the story of the making of the Golden Calf in Exod. 32. 25–29. The reference to the disowning of parents reflects a form of legal separation and implies that the service of God overrides all ties of family and kinship. The *covenant* referred to must be the covenant between God and Israel, and not a special covenant entrusting the priesthood to Levi.

As custodians of the Ark of the Covenant and administrators of matters relating to worship the Levites were the guides and teachers of Israel more generally (v. 10). As worship became more narrowly focused on one single sanctuary, in accordance with Deuteronomy's ruling, the role of the Levites appears to have broadened considerably. They became Israel's teachers on all matters concerning the knowledge and worship of the LORD as the God of Israel.

The reference to adversaries and the call to God to assist in striking down those who opposed Levi (v. 11) is surprising. No fuller explanation of this hostility is forthcoming and this has led to the suggestion that this verse may originally have been located after v. 5 where it applies to Judah, or possibly one of the other tribes. Those settled east of the River Jordan were constantly threatened, and soon overwhelmed, by their non-Israelite neighbours.

33. 12 *Benjamin* Benjamin was Jacob's youngest son and was particularly loved by his father (Gen. 44. 20). The reference to *the High God* rests on a reconstruction of the probable original text (cf. margin, following the ancient Greek). *Under his protection* is literally 'between his shoulders' (as NRSV), but understood as a reference to mountains (cf. Num. 34. 11; Jos. 15. 8). The name Benjamin means 'Southerner', but was understood from their settlement to the south of the central highlands of Ephraim and Manasseh.

33.13 *Joseph* The Joseph tribe incorporated the two tribes of Ephraim and Manasseh (cf. v. 17 and Num. 1. 10; 26. 28) which are elsewhere frequently noted separately. They occupied the rich and fertile region of the central highlands, which is the chief feature of their existence noted in the blessing here. Their position made them the most powerful of those tribes settled in the centre and north of the land, and also marked them out as the strongest rival to Judah in the south. The rejection of the dynastic rule of the Davidic royal house after Solomon's death (I Kgs. 12. 1–24) owed much to this long-felt rivalry between Ephraim and Judah.

The title *him who dwells in the burning bush* (v. 16) alludes to the revelation of God to Moses in the burning bush recounted in Exod. 3. 1–15. Some commentators have suggested emending the Hebrew word for 'bush' to 'Sinai' (as in NRSV), but there is no textual evidence for such a change.

The popular image of the bull as a symbol of power and vitality (v. 17) is widely used, but there may be a narrower point to the reference here in view of the popularity of the bull-calves as symbols of divinity in Bethel – the leading sanctuary of the tribe of Ephraim. Hostility to this image is frequently expressed (cf. I Kgs. 12. 28–30).

33. 18 *Zebulun and Issachar* The saying includes the two tribes of Zebulun (or Zebulon, NRSV) and Issachar which were settled in the region in the far north of the land, close to the famous Phoenician seaports of Tyre and Sidon. Zebulun was associated with the seaborne trade of its Phoenician neighbours, which explains the significance of *when you set forth* (i.e. 'put to sea'), while Issachar remained ashore living in tents.

The mountain referred to in v. 19 was evidently the location of a sanctuary, probably that on Mount Tabor (cf. Judg. 4. 6, 12). The close relationship with the Phoenicians (the inventors of a written alphabet) provided a major cultural and trading link for early Israel, but the

147

vulnerability of the region to later Mesopotamian incursions brought disastrous consequences (cf. Isa. 9. 1).

33. 20–21 *Gad* The tribe of Gad proved itself to be the strongest of the tribes settled on the east of Jordan and became renowned for its military prowess (vv. 20–21). This explains its lionlike qualities singled out here.

33. 22 *Dan* Dan formed the most northerly of Israel's tribes and, like Gad, was renowned for its fierce character – a quality vital for defending its territory which was located at the intersection of vital trading routes.

33. 23 *Naphtali* NRSV understands the reference to the 'sea' (i.e. the Mediterranean) to indicate the western coastland more generally. However the precise areas of territory occupied by the various tribes cannot be determined with accuracy and, in any event, certainly changed considerably over a period of time. The link between a tribe and its territory was a powerful and deeply emotional one.

33. 24–25 *Asher* The tribe of Asher was settled on the rich northern coastland, famed for its olives. Accordingly the poetic word-imagery used in this blessing indicates prosperity and rich olive harvests (vv. 24–25). The concluding plea is for Asher to have the strength to defend its wealth.

The portrayal of God riding on the clouds (v. 26) as his heavenly chariot to come to the aid of Israel (Jeshurun) is also found in some psalms (cf. Ps. 18. 10; 68. 33, etc.) and links closely with similar descriptions of the god Baal found in Canaanite sources.

The text of v. 27 rests on an emendation, but the reference appears to be to the victories granted to Israel at the beginning of its national story which enabled them to take possession of their land. Finally Moses' Farewell Blessing looks forward to Israel's increased prosperity, but recognizes that this will continue to entice enemies to attack, so that a strong defence will remain necessary.

From a preacher's perspective much that is most striking in the Blessing of Moses lies in its emphasis upon material prosperity and abundant harvests – the very causes of the temptation to spiritual complacency of which Deuteronomy has repeatedly warned. God is not indifferent to material needs, but recognizes their temporary, and vulnerable, nature. More valuable in the poem is the emphasis upon the variety of the gifts and benefits which the several tribes of Israel will possess. It comes consistently as a matter of surprise to visitors to the land of Israel that such great variations of climate, landscape and life-styles can co-exist in so small a strip of land. From the semi-tropical forests of Dan to the desert of Beersheba it becomes evident that God does not seek a dull uniformity.

From the perspective of a Christian preacher this farewell Blesssing of Moses invites close comparison with the Farewell Prayer of Jesus for his disciples in John 17. 1–26. Many of the same issues appear in each of them: the sense of handing over a trust, awareness of the people's vulnerability to the dangers and temptations that they will face, and the longing to be with them in their time of trial. The speech and the prayer commit to God's care a people facing a challenging and difficult future.

The death of Moses
34. 1–12

The concluding chapter of the book consists of a short historical summary in vv. 1–6 which rounds off the story of Moses and Israel's wilderness years, preparing for the new era which begins in the book of Joshua with the story of the crossing of the Jordan and the entry into the land. The age of revelation, in its primary form, is at an end and an age under a new order is about to begin. Two short notes then mark the handing-over of the duties of leadership to Joshua (vv. 7–9) and a summarizing review of all that Moses has meant for the birth of Israel in vv. 10–12. The use of both names for the mountain which Moses ascended in order to see the land in v. 1 – Nebo (cf. 32. 49) and Pisgah (cf. 3. 27) – points to their essential identity. That Moses 'saw' the whole land of Israel was important for establishing the extent of the territory to which Israel laid claim. It may also be argued that this act of 'showing the land' was intended to have the legal force of granting possession. Much discussion has focused on the historical validity of this claim, whether it represents an 'idealized' Deuteronomic ambition, or reflects more substantially the area of land which at one time formed part of the 'Greater Israel' over which king David ruled. No clear answer can be given, and it is certain that the territorial boundaries, tribal affiliations and political administration of the entire region remained in a constant state of flux from the early second millennium BCE until Roman times.

149

The fact that the site of Moses' burial was unknown (vv. 5–6) marks an important feature of the tradition that this great leader belonged to 'all Israel' and not to one tribe, or region, as king David had done. Clearly there were no pilgrimages to the site of Moses' tomb, and the most that could be achieved was to journey south to the holy mountain of Horeb, as Elijah had done (I Kgs. 19. 8–9). In 31. 2 Moses recognizes that his strength was failing and that he was no longer able to lead Israel, which rather contrasts with the eulogy of his great strength into old age given in vv. 7–8. Cf. Num. 33. 39 for Aaron's death at the age of 123. A similar length of mourning for Aaron is noted in Num. 20. 29.

The suitability of Joshua to be the successor of Moses is set out more fully in Num. 27. 18–23. That Moses had 'seen' God, insofar as this was at all possible, is described in Exod. 33. 11 and that he was a unique prophet is affirmed in Num. 12. 6–8. There is a measure of divine authority implicit in the reference in the final verses 11–12 to the signs and portents which Moses displayed before Pharaoh (cf. also 4. 34).